The **Essential** Buyer's Guide

PEUGEOT

205 GTI

Your marque expert:
Jon Blackburn

VELOCE PUBLISHING
THE PUBLISHER OF FINE AUTOMOTIVE BOOKS

Also from Veloce –

Veloce's Essential Buyer's Guide Series
Alfa Romeo Giulia GT (Booker)
Alfa Romeo Spider Giulia (Booker & Talbott)
Austin Seven (Barker)
BMW GS (Henshaw)
BSA Bantam (Henshaw)
BSA 500 & 650 Twins (Henshaw)
Citroën 2CV (Paxton)
Citroën ID & DS (Heilig)
Corvette C2 1963-1967 (Falconer)
Fiat 500 & 600 (Bobbitt)
Ford Capri (Paxton)
Harley-Davidson Big Twins (Henshaw)
Hinckley Triumph triples & fours 750, 900, 955,
    1000, 1050, 1200 – 1991-2009 (Henshaw)
Honda CBR600 (Henshaw)
Honda FireBlade (Henshaw)
Honda SOHC fours (Henshaw)
Jaguar E-type 3.8 & 4.2-litre (Crespin)
Jaguar E-type V12 5.3-litre (Crespin)
Jaguar XJ 1995-2003 (Crespin)
Jaguar/Daimler XJ6, XJ12 & Sovereign (Crespin)
Jaguar/Daimler XJ40 (Crespin)
Jaguar XJ-S (Crespin)
Jaguar XK8 (Thorley)
Land Rover Series I, II & IIA (Thurman)
MG Midget & A-H Sprite (Horler)
MG TD & TF (Jones)
MGB & MGB GT (Williams)
Mercedes-Benz 280SL-560DSL Roadsters (Bass)
Mercedes-Benz 'Pagoda' 230SL, 250SL & 280SL
    Roadsters & Coupés (Bass)
Mini (Paxton)
Morris Minor & 1000 (Newell)
Norton Commando (Henshaw)
Porsche 911 SC (Streather)
Porsche 911 (964) (Streather)
Porsche 911 (993) (Streather)
Porsche 911 (996) (Streather)
Porsche 928 (Hemmings)
Rolls-Royce Silver Shadow & Bentley T-Series (Bobbitt)
Subaru Impreza (Hobbs)
Triumph Bonneville (Henshaw)
Triumph Spitfire & GT6 (Baugues)
Triumph Stag (Mort & Fox)

Triumph TR6 (Williams)
Triumph TR7 & TR8 (Williams)
Vespa Scooters (Paxton)
VW Beetle (Cservenka & Copping)
VW Bus (Cservenka & Copping)
VW Golf GTI (Cservenka & Copping)

From Veloce Publishing's new imprints:

Soviet General and field rank officer uniforms:
    1955 to 1991 (Streather)
Soviet military and paramilitary services: female
    uniforms 1941-1991 (Streather)

Animal Grief – How animals mourn for each other (Alderton)
Clever Dog! (O'Meara)
Complete Dog Massage Manual, The – Gentle Dog Care
    (Robertson)
Dinner with Rover (Paton-Ayre)
Dog Cookies (Schops)
Dog Games – Stimulating play to entertain your dog and
    you (Blenski)
Dog Relax – Relaxed dogs, relaxed owners (Pilguj)
Exercising your puppy: a gentle & natural approach – Gentle
    Dog Care (Robertson)
Fun and games for cats (Seidl)
Know Your Dog – The guide to a beautiful relationship
    (Birmelin)
Living with an Older Dog – Gentle Dog Care (Alderton & Hall)
My dog has cruciate ligament injury – but lives life to the full!
    (Häusler)
My dog has hip dysplasia – but lives life to the full! (Häusler)
My dog is blind – but lives life to the full! (Horsky)
My dog is deaf – but lives life to the full! (Willms)
Smellorama – nose games for dogs (Theby)
Swim to Recovery: Canine hydrotherapy healing (Wong
Waggy Tails & Wheelchairs (Epp)
Walking the dog – motorway walks for drivers and dogs
    (Rees)
Winston ... the dog who changed my life (Klute)
You and Your Border Terrier – The Essential Guide (Alderton)
You and Your Cockapoo – The Essential Guide (Alderton)

www.veloce.co.uk

First published in May 2011 by Veloce Publishing Limited, Veloce House, Parkway Farm Business Park, Middle Farm Way,
Poundbury, Dorchester, Dorset, DT1 3AR, England. Fax 01305 250479/
e-mail info@veloce.co.uk/web www.veloce.co.uk or www.velocebooks.com.

ISBN: 978-1-845842-83-3 UPC: 6-36847-04283-7

British Library Cataloguing in Publication Data – A catalogue record for this book is available from the British Library.
Typesetting, design and page make-up all by Veloce Publishing Ltd on Apple Mac.
Printed in India by Imprint Digital.

Introduction
– the purpose of this book

Introduction

The purpose of this book is to offer a step-by-step guide to assessing a 205 GTI or CTI Cabriolet. Whether you're looking to buy a weekend car or a restoration project, the 205 could be the car for you. Armed with the information and guidance in this book you should be able to buy with confidence and negotiate a fair price.

The 205 GTI, with its lightweight, pin-sharp handling, and punchy engine, is still the benchmark against which new GTIs are measured. It's now more affordable than ever and, since its birth, its cult status has ensured it will remain a future classic. CTIs are also becoming rare and more sought-after.

The World Championship-winning 205 Turbo 16 rally car. (Courtesy Guy Loveridge)

The 205 GTI – the birth of an icon

In the early '80s, the UK recession changed the public's perception of small cars from being economical to fashionable. In response, Peugeot designed the stylish 205 to appeal to drivers considering moving to a smaller car, but it had no idea how successful it would be.

In 1984, the 205 1.6 GTI arrived, helping to change Peugeot's 'stuffy' image forever, and set a new benchmark for hot hatches eight years after the legendary Golf GTI. Resembling the brutal World Rally Championship winning 205 Turbo 16 rally car – with 14-inch Speedline alloys, body decals, grey body mouldings, front foglights, and rear spoiler – it let other road uses know what they were dealing with.

With the T16 winning rallies, Ford's saying "race on Sunday, sell on Monday" was never truer, and demand soared. Peugeot dealers never needed to offer discount on a sale, and the 205 became a favourite with the motoring press, being one of the best drives for the money. They loved its rev-happy engine, sharp handling, involving steering, and (alleged) Pininfarina styling. *Autocar* even referred to it as the Mini

Cooper of the '80s. Not only did it look good, with performance to embarrass more expensive cars, it was practical, too.

In 1986, a retuned engine kept up with the competition, and the soft top CTI Cabriolet was launched – so you could now have your cake, and eat it!

As much fun as you can handle

Peugeot got serious in 1986, launching the 1.9 GTI, capable of 0-60mph in 7.8 seconds! Whereas the 1.6 was applauded for its precise and playable nature, the 1.9 was its 'evil brother,' needing to be handled with respect. Launched with the slogan 'Hot cat on a tin-roof,' its 15-inch Speedline alloys and half-leather seats gave the car a more purposeful look. Peugeot even specified 98 RON Super petrol signalling the car's intent.

The original 205 GTI icon. Peugeot's advertising slogan was, "If you want something sensible – buy an anorak!" (Courtesy Peugeot)

Hot hatches were, and still are, manufactured with safety in mind, understeering when the limits of control are reached. Peugeot, on the other hand, produced a front-wheel drive car that, in the hands of a skilled driver, could be as much fun as a rear-wheel drive car. The addictive oversteer could be invoked by entering a corner fast, lifting off the accelerator mid-bend, and then reapplying to catch the slide. Thus, the 205 quickly gained a reputation for sudden lift-off oversteer, ready to catch out inexperienced drivers.

With the 205 GTI leading the way, over 5 million 205s were sold worldwide, transforming Peugeot's fortunes from near bankruptcy to market leader. Modern safety legislation means a car like the focused 205 GTI would never be built today (more's the pity). Many argue that Peugeot has yet to produce a worthy successor, and, as a result, mint 205 GTIs are now highly sought-after.

Happy hunting.

Thanks
Alan Jarrett – Sales Manager (1983-2002), Dealer Principle (2002-2005), Bugeons Motors (Peugeot dealership), Shrewsbury, Shropshire
Dave Goddard – Pugs@Pool Peugeot Club
Graham Phillips
Miles@PugRacing
http://forum.205gtidrivers.com online forum – Cybernck, Anthony and photo contributors

Essential Buyer's Guide™ currency

At the time of publication a BG unit of currency "●" equals approximately £1.00/US$1.60/Euro 1.19. Please adjust to current exchange rates using £1.00 as the datum.

Contents

1 Is it the right car for you?
– marriage guidance

Will I fit behind the wheel?
There's plenty of fore/aft seat adjustment. However, if you're very tall you should check there's enough headroom.

Will it fit the garage?
It will fit most single garages, although the 3-door shell's large doors need to be opened fairly wide to enable passengers to get in and out of the back seats comfortably.

Interior space
Room for four adults. With wheels as close to the car's corners as possible, it offers a 'big car' feel, and (unlike its contemporaries) minimal front wheelarch intrusion enables the pedals to be placed directly in front of the driver, offset to the right or left.

The CTI has very large sills, which intrude into the footwells.

50/50 split folding rear seats mean even a GTI can be practical.

Luggage capacity
The rear seats fold flat creating a generous load bay (42ft^3 in the GTI), with no intrusion from rear suspension. The CTI has no hatch, but does have enough room for a couple of bags for those weekends away.

Running costs
Typical fuel consumption is around 27-31mpg (miles per gallon) for combined driving. For a 1.9 GTI it's 30mpg. 1.6 GTIs are a touch more frugal, and CTIs fall between the two. Automatics are very thirsty. Early GTIs require 98 RON fuel.

Usability
All are very usable, keeping pace with modern traffic, and comfortable for long trips, especially the 1.9 GTI with its longer gearing. 1.6 GTIs are 'buzzy' at motorway speeds; the 1.9 GTI is a very capable car; CTIs are less practical in winter.

Parts availability
Most spares are available from motor factors and aftermarket specialists (listed on page 58). Peugeot still stock some genuine parts, although sadly its stock is declining. Secondhand parts are becoming more costly and harder to find.

Parts cost
Service items are reasonable, and branded parts are recommended (Bosch, etc). Some genuine Peugeot parts are expensive – electrical items such as an airflow meter (AFM), switchgear, and window motors. Rare trim parts for special editions and CTIs are expensive and difficult to find.

Insurance group
Due to the GTI's reputation (crashes by inexperienced drivers and thefts) insurance premiums are high: 1.9 GTIs are (UK) group 16! However, classic car limited mileage policies are available. Owners' clubs often have a discount with specific insurers.

Investment potential
Future classic. There are still plenty about, but prices are rising. CTIs and special editions are getting rare. Bargain GTIs can be picked up if you're handy with a spanner – although it's worth holding out for a good one.

The 205 GTI: a great driver's car. (Courtesy Dale Mills)

Foibles
- Essential to check for accident damage and repair on GTIs.
- Rear beam bearings seize.
- Leaky interiors and damp carpets.
- Head gasket failure.
- 'Mayonnaise' in the oil filler cap (see chapter 7).
- 'Lumpy' idle and stalling problems (especially early phase 1 cars).

Plus points
Design has aged very well. Reputation, handling, and performance. Galvanised shell means rust problems are limited – rare in a classic car! Most parts easily obtained.

Minus points
Hard ride (GTI) and cheap interiors: noisy cabin, with rattles and creaking dash ("they all do that Sir!"). Unassisted steering is heavy at parking speeds; poor heaters; front seat wear; thin body panels vulnerable to damage; and poor urban fuel consumption. Some are distastefully modified and/or thrashed.

Alternatives
'80s rivals include:

1.6 GTI
Ford Fiesta XR2 and Escort XR3
MkI VW Golf GTI
Vauxhall Nova GSi
Fiat Uno Turbo

CTI
MkI VW Golf Cabriolet
Escort Cabriolet
Astra/Kadett Cabriolet

1.9 GTI
Peugeot 309 GTI
Ford RS Escort
MkII 16-valve VW Golf GTI
Renault 5 Turbo
Vauxhall Astra GTE

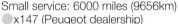

Small service: 6000 miles (9656km)
●x147 (Peugeot dealership)
Large service: 12,000 miles (19,312km)
●x278 (Peugeot dealership)

New clutch (fitted): ●x92
Rebuilt engine: ●x400-800 in parts
Secondhand engine: ●x150-250
Rebuilt gearbox: ●x250+
Secondhand

A seized rear beam is costly to fix. (Courtesy Mark Dixon)

gearbox: ●x50-100
Unleaded head conversion: n/a

Front brake disc: ●x22 each
Front brake disc pad set: ●x18
Rear brake disc: ●x20 each
Rear brake disc pad set: ●x21
Rear brake drum: ●x56 each
Rear brake shoes: ●x18
Front suspension arm (inc ball joint): ●x57 per side
Drop link: ●x17 each
Track rod end: ●x15 each
Front wheel bearings: ●x16 each
Rear stub axle: ●x46 each
Rear arm: ●x63 each
Driveshaft: ●x53 each (plus refundable surcharge ●x25)
Replacement fully refurbished rear beam: ●x350+

Door lock set: ●x44
Headlight: ●x27
Front driving lamps: ●x34
Genuine front wing: ●x65
Body seals set: ●x163
Hood/soft top: ●x454

Complete body restoration: ●x4000+
Full respray (inc preparation): ●x2000+
Full professional restoration from basket case: ●x8000+

Parts that are easy to find
Body panels, service and mechanical parts, most body seals, and glass.

Parts that are hard to find
Correct exhaust system and windscreen rubber with sunroof wind deflector on top lip. Interior/trim from CTIs, special editions, and early cars.

Parts that are very expensive
CTI door rubbers ●x250 each; CTI window seals ●x120 each; Bosch fuel relay ●x70; electric window motors ●x131; set of new bumpers and exterior trim ●x150; rear beam trailing arm bearings – parts ●x125 – fitted (specialist equipment required) ●x600 dealer bill is typical.

Labour costs not included unless specified.

Peugeot's down pipe (available from Arvin/Timax ch16). Budget exhausts don't have the 2 into 1 section and reduce hp. (Courtesy Andrew Westrop)

Special edition interiors such as this Griffe can be expensive and hard to find. (Courtesy Carl Chambers)

3 Living with a Peugeot 205 GTI or CTI
– will you get along together?

Both the 205 GTI and CTI are capable of keeping pace with modern cars. The body styling has aged well, and with a variety of extras, special editions, and engine sizes you should be able to find a car that satisfies both your budget and your needs. CTIs offered an interesting blend of sporty motoring and top-down driving. It was only available as a 3-door model but, despite this, it was surprisingly practical, with generous 50:50 split rear seats, and a very usable boot.

The 205's mechanicals are robust if serviced regularly, and engines last well if looked after, but can go out of tune. An excellent network of specialists and online forums provides valuable advice and support.

What to expect?
When you get into the car you're initially greeted by gaudy red '80s-style carpets and a plastic interior. However, it feels roomy for a small car, and the controls are well placed. Start the engine and the lumpy idle and exhaust note give a clue to the cars intent.

What is it like to drive?
On the move, with little sound proofing, rattles, and a creaking dash, you may wonder what you've let yourself in for, but the GTI's driving experience is legendary for good reason: few cars can match its shear 'chuckability' and rawness.

GTI boot: with the rear seats folded it offers a generous load bay.

Both the revvy 1.6 and the torquey 1.9 engines provide enough excitement for road or track. The 1.9 is better suited to everyday use, the extra torque requiring fewer gear changes in traffic, and taller gearing for more relaxed motorway cruising. Inexperienced drivers may find it more difficult to drive, but with no electronic driving aids (and its tendency to oversteer on the limit when backing off the throttle mid-bend) it's ultimately more rewarding than modern day counterparts. The 1.9's larger 15-inch wheels have higher cornering limits and hold the road better, too, but rear-end step-out is less gradual than on the 1.6s, and slow speed manoeuvring is harder (although power steering was optional). Where road compromises are not an issue, GTIs can be modified, with tuning and suspension upgrades being popular.

To this day the 205 GTI is still mentioned in group car tests of new GTIs, and with good reason. A good 205 GTI should be a fun drive, and whilst modern equivalents may produce more power, most won't have the raw, addictive grin factor. Most cars are now over 20 years old, however, and bad ones can be dogs, with tired interiors and engines. Yet find a good one and you can enjoy pin-sharp handling, strong brakes, and a punchy engine which is hard to beat for the money.

CTI Cabriolet
The CTI is a comfortable car for two people plus luggage, with later cars benefitting from a power hood and power steering. As with all soft tops, it's vulnerable to vandalism, and old hoods are prone to leaks. The hood is quick in use and very

low when folded down, giving good visibility. However, when up, the large C-pillars reduce visibility when overtaking and reverse parking. Wind noise is louder than the GTI and the interior can be cold in winter.

Although the '80s design has more scuttle shake than modern cabriolets, and the large strengthening sills intrude into the footwells, it does have the 50:50 split rear seats, making it one of the most practical cabriolets you can buy. Rear passengers have wind-down windows – never available on the GTI.

Despite the extra chassis strengthening required for a cabriolet, adding over 100kg and dulling engine performance, a lower centre of gravity means it's no slouch around the corners. Being more softly sprung than the GTIs, it's also more comfortable.

On a sunny day the unique Pininfarina-styled practical classic might fit the bill. Although the CTI lacks the ultimate speed and usability of the GTI, it's a small price to pay for top-down, practical motoring.

Practicalities – will it suit your lifestyle?

I use my 205 1.9 GTI daily, and the car has completed over 200,000 miles with its

original engine. I've owned it for 6 years and, as well as regular servicing, I've replaced the rear beam and fitted uprated bushes; rebushed the front wishbones; replaced the driver's sill; and fitted uprated suspension. 205s are relatively simple to repair: the tricky bits are the rear beam and the engine management/injection system, which can become tired and in need of attention.

The car has only broken down twice (a faulty fuel relay, and a starter motor), and I enjoy driving it today just as much as the day I first bought it. Its simplicity and rewarding drive are an attractive combination.

Choose wisely and a good GTI should make you smile on twisty B-roads; any foibles will soon be forgiven!

CTI boot with rear seats folded. (Courtesy Stuart Farrimond)

The CTI – a soft top that's affordable, practical and sporty: it doesn't get any better than this. (Courtesy Stuart Farrimond)

4 Relative values
– which model for you?

The original 205 GTI. The best all-rounder, some would argue (especially the 115bhp version), but becoming harder to find in good condition. (Courtesy Ed Cherry)

The 205 had a long production run, so, whether it's an early original car or a special edition loaded with extras, you should be able to find what you're after.

It never received a comprehensive face-lift, but there were a number of design and styling revisions – known as 'phases' – which affected all GTIs and CTIs (detailed below under 1.6 GTI, to avoid repetition).

The 122bhp 1.9GTI = **100%**

1.6 GTI April 1984-September 1992

The original 1.6 GTI (105bhp) was – and still is – a beautifully balanced mix of power and handling: a 0-60mph dash in 9.5 seconds and top speed of 118mph.

The original 1.6 GTI phase 1 interior with red carpeting, Biarritz cloth seats, linear heater controls, and '80s-style alarm. (Courtesy Ed Cherry)

Phase 1 1.9 GTIs benefited from Quattro velour half leather seats. (Courtesy Dale Mills)

Phase 1: the original sporty interior's dashboard had linear heater controls, recessed dials, 2-spoke steering wheel with GTI lettering, red and black Biarritz velour seats, red carpeting, and a 4-speaker stereo. Externally, twin long-range driving lamps were mounted in a deep front spoiler, and the large grey side mouldings and bumper had red inserts. The C-pillar had twin '1.6' and 'GTI' decals (a theme continued on all models), 14-inch pepper pot alloys, bronze-tinted windscreen, and a rear wash/wiper. Central locking was optional. Body colours included alpine white, cherry red, graphite grey, silver, and black. In January 1986 rear seatbelts were fitted.

In April 1986, a big valve head from the 1.9 GTI, and revised camshaft, raised the power to 115bhp: 0-60mph was reduced to 9.1 seconds and top speed increased to 121mph. Suspension dampening and springs were also softened. In June, side repeater indicators and leather-bound steering wheel were added, along with revised instrumentation. Electric windows and sliding glass sunroof were optional.

Phase 1.5, January 1988: the entire range received revised trim including a new style dash with rotary heater controls, revised dials, 3-spoke steering wheel with GTI lettering, and Monaco tweed seat trim. Although Peugeot had begun to use phase

Phase 1.5 interior with new rotary heater controls and restyled Quartet velour black and red seats – again all-cloth in the 1.6, and half-leather in the 1.9 GTI (pictured) – continued until production ended.

1.5 parts leading up to the official change date. The GTI's new rear spoiler was now screwed on, not glued, and had rounded, not square, ends. The internally adjusted wing mirrors were larger, with a flat-shaped base taking over from the previously rounded design. These are all good pointers to identifying a genuine early model, or if these parts have been replaced. Metallic paint was optional.

In August 1989, Quartet velour black and red seats with plain black velour side supports became standard, along with carpeted boot and central locking. The BE-1 gearbox, criticised for a heavy clutch, was replaced with an improved BE-3 gearbox, with reverse positioned bottom-right, opposite 5th gear. By October '89 power steering became an option. In March 1990 the ignition coil was relocated to the inlet manifold.

Phase 2, September 1990: changes included new black exterior bumper and side trim, new clear front indicator lenses, smoked rear lenses, with the reverse light moved to the rear bumper. The dashboard, door plastics and window/door seals were darkened, and anti-lock brakes (ABS) became an option on the GTI. The expansion tank and thermostat housing were also changed to create space for the ABS pump.

In October 1991, a lights on warning buzzer and remote central locking became standard, and air-conditioning was an option. However catalytic convertors were never an option on the UK 1.6 GTI.

Value: 1.6 GTI 105bhp = **70%** (the car that started it all: sadly most have worn interiors and high mileage now); 115bhp = **80%** (probably the best 1.6 GTI.)

Phase 2 1.6 GTI all-cloth interior. Note the darkened plastics and trim. (Courtesy Michael Cockbain)

1.9 GTI December 1986-April 1994

Although similar to the 1.6 GTI, the 1.9 GTI, the larger stroked engine had a rather different nature: with a wide, flat torque curve giving a more 'grown up' car, the 130bhp 1905cc engine and revised gear ratios enabled 0-60 in 7.8 seconds, and a top speed of 127mph.

Electric windows, central locking, Quattro velour half-leather seats, and sought-after 15in Speedline wheels (later replaced with SMRs) were fitted. Other changes included an oil cooler, larger front callipers, solid discs replacing rear drums, strengthened driveshafts (necessitating different hubs with larger wheel bearings), and stiffened suspension with larger ARBs (anti-roll bars).

In addition to the 1.6 GTI phase changes, 1989 saw the seats changed

Peugeot gets serious: the 1.9GTI – an '80s hot hatch performance benchmark. (Courtesy David Sykes)

to black and red Quartet velour, and a slightly larger exhaust fitted. A sliding glass sunroof was optional.

In October 1992, emissions laws resulted in the XU9JAZ 122bhp catalysed engine becoming mandatory. Lower compression ratio (9:2) and revised camshaft profile dulled performance, with a 0-60 time of 8.5 seconds and 125mph top speed. However, superior engine management resulted in a smoother idle, reduced part-throttle kangarooing, and enabled the use of either 95 RON or 98 RON fuel. The ECU can also be remapped. Grey carpet and power-assisted steering became standard.

Value: 1.9 GTI 130bhp = **90%** (still sought-after but most are very high mileage); 122bhp = **100%** (newer, slightly slower, but smoother engines and more modern interiors).

CTI Cabriolet June 1986-April 1994
More expensive than the GTI, the CTI didn't sell well. Launched with a 115bhp 1.6 GTI engine, it gave a creditable 0-60 of 10.1 seconds and a 115mph top speed. Colours included white, red, silver, graphite grey, and haze (metallic) blue.

In 1988 the dashboard was revised (as per phase 1.5 changes) and red GTI

CTIs are slowly increasing in value and are at bargain prices: fun, cheap to run, and one of the most practical cabriolets you can buy. (Courtesy Peugeot)

fabric door stripes were added, but seats remained trimmed in Biarritz velour when the GTI changed to Monaco tweed. In August, new colours included ivory white (replacing Haze blue), scarlet red, silver, and graphite grey. Power steering became optional from October. In 1990, Quartet velour seats, central locking, front electric windows, and metallic paint were introduced. Atlantic blue paint was optional, and (previously optional) electric power hoods became standard from September.

In October 1991, the de-tuned (105bhp) 1.9lt XU9J1/Z catalysed engine was introduced to meet emission regulations, dulling 0-60 performance to 10.6 seconds. Air-conditioning became an option, and most CTIs were now alpine white or scarlet red.

Value: **65%** (manual hood); **75%** (power hood). Becoming rarer and more desirable, but it still doesn't rival the price of an equivalent age and condition 1.9 GTI. Hood condition greatly affects the price. Due to the nature of the car, low mileage examples are easier to find than GTIs.

205 GTI special editions
October 1990 Miami blue & Sorrento green Limited Edition (LE)
With Miami blue or Sorrento green paintwork (new colours at the time), power steering, grey full leather seats, matching grey carpets and mats, it's very desirable. When new, it sold at a 20% premium over standard GTIs – and still does. Paint colours were also available for standard models, too, so check it's a genuine LE.

Value: 1.9 GTI = **120%**
1.6 GTI = **115%**.

The Miami blue 1.9GTI – one of the nicest colours available. Note the clear indicators and black body trim, common to all late models.
(Courtesy Michael Cockbain)

Sorrento green: also a desirable colour.
(Courtesy Mark Dixon)

The Griffe came fitted with all the factory options. (Courtesy Carl Chambers)

1990 Griffe 1.9 GTI

The Griffe (French for claw) was named to link with Peugeot's lion motif. Identified by 'Laser' green paint, mid-grey bumper inserts (normally red), black carpets, dark grey anodised alloy wheels with a silver rim, full black leather interior, ABS, power-assisted steering, and a sunroof.

Value: **200%** upwards – price on condition due to rarity, although most were imported left-hand drive.

March 1992/93 – 205 Gentry

The Gentry: very nicely trimmed, but the engine is disappointing.

Although not strictly a GTI, the Gentry was available in Sorrento green and Aztec gold (or Beige Mayfair – an acquired taste!). Its luxurious interior included: full leather seats (tan or black), leather-trimmed steering wheel, polished wood door inserts, grey velour carpets, illuminated sunvisor vanity mirrors, electric heated wing mirrors, electric windows (which worked with the ignition off) and power-assisted steering. GTI red inserts on the side trim and bumper were replaced with chrome, and 14in alloy wheels came from the GTX model. However, with its thirsty 4-speed automatic, and de-tuned catalysed engine, it's not generally sought-after by GTI enthusiasts. Although, the Sorrento version is a popular choice for manual engine conversions.

Value: **85%**

October 1992/93 – 25 'Radio 1FM' models

The Radio 1FM model commemorated 25 years of Radio 1 broadcasting, with an on-air competition to win a car. All 25 were individually numbered with a small brass plate, and had unique 'Radio 1FM 25th' bodywork decals and special badging. It had black body paint, and dark grey

Radio 1FM: very rare and worth collecting if you can find one.

alloy wheels with silver rim. It also had every extra, including power steering, ABS, sliding sunroof, immobiliser, remote central locking, air-conditioning, full black leather seats, luxury grey carpet, and special Radio 1FM mats. Appropriately for this model, an upgraded, four-speaker Clarion stereo system with remote six-disc CD auto-changer was also fitted. There's even a website dedicated to the model (chapter 16).

Value: **200% upwards** – price on condition due to rarity.

1992 1.9 GTI Export Automatic

The GTI automatic was a cancelled order intended for Japan. Despite being available in right-hand drive and having air-conditioning, it's not sought-after by GTI enthusiasts due to its thirsty, 4-speed automatic and de-tuned catalysed engine. It has 1.6 GTI running gear and interior, with 14in wheels.

1.9 GTI Automatic: note the different dash gauges, with incremental numbers, and extra push switches below the heater controls. (Courtesy Mick Lawton)

The jack is relocated under the front seat, as the air-con unit inhabits its usual place in the engine bay. Interestingly, the accelerator pedal has a block attached to it, to bring the pedal closer to the driver.

Value: **75%** upwards – difficult to price as they are rarely for sale. Buy for its rarity, not performance.

Rare paintwork

Although not a special edition, a GTI Topaz blue colour was introduced for a short time in 1990, and Laser green metallic paint was an option for 12 months in 1991. From September 1990 Steel grey was available, with black and green Quartet velour seats, and dark green carpet.

Value: standard model **plus 15%**.

A GTI in Topaz blue – a very rare colour. (Courtesy Rob King)

Dimma wide-body conversions

Inspired by the T16 Rally Car, the £5000 drive-in 160 man-hour Dimma conversion would totally transform your car, and it was also factory approved. It consisted of huge vented wheelarches, flared front wings, deep front air-dam, vented bonnet, revised tailgate, huge roof spoiler, and special wheels. Full leather seats and lowered suspension were also an option. CTI conversions were very rare.

Dimmas were sometimes complemented by a Turbo Technics conversion, giving

The T16-inspired Dimma wide-body conversion gave the 205 GTI a whole new profile … (Courtesy Mike Bullock)

… and it even has an identity plate. (Courtesy Mike Bullock)

the car the performance to match its looks, and other tuners, such as Guttmann, offered similar 'race look' kits in the '90s.

Value: depending on condition, typical minimum value of standard model **plus 50%** (eg 1.9 GTI 122bhp = 100 + 50 = **150%**); Replacement wheels are very expensive.

Turbo Technics (TT) conversions

In the late '80s, TT offered a £2500 drive-in conversion for your GTI. With the addition of a Garret T25 turbocharger, front mounted intercooler, larger oil cooler, skimmed pistons, and a supplemental ECU-controlled 5th injector in the throttle body, the performance was stunning. A 115bhp 1.6 GTI increased to 160bhp with 162lbf/ft of torque. The 1.9 GTI was even more impressive, increasing from 130bhp to 175bhp, with a massive 182lbf/ft of torque at 3000rpm – slashing the usual 7.8 second 0-60mph to 6.3 seconds, with a top speed of 132mph! The 1.9 conversion required an uprated clutch, larger exhaust system, and a two-stage boost controller on the dashboard – medium or high boost (0.65bar). Guttmann offered a similar conversion in the early '90s.

Value: depending on condition, typical value of at least the existing car **plus 50%**. Be wary of tired or worn engines. A replacement turbo manifold is very expensive (●x250). Look for TT badging on the tailgate and wing, and an identification plate in the engine bay.

Rare TT plus Dimma conversion: standard model **plus 100%**.

The Turbo Technics Dimma 205 GTI: a very rare conversion, but provides serious power! Modified front bodywork accommodates the larger oil cooler and intercooler. (Courtesy Mark Rushton)

TT conversion, with an aftermarket dump valve and air filter. (Courtesy Daniel Davies)

A popular induction mod was to alter the air intake system to give a shorter route to the turbo, and prevent hot air being sucked in above the turbo and exhaust manifold. (Courtesy Mark Rushton)

5 Before you view

– be well informed

To avoid a wasted journey, and the disappointment of finding that the car doesn't match your expectations, it will help if you're very clear about what questions you want to ask before you pick up the telephone. Some of these might appear basic but when you're excited about the prospect of buying your dream classic, it's amazing how things slip the mind ... Also, check the current values of the model you're interested in in classic car magazines, which give both a price guide and auction results.

Where is the car?

Is it going to be worth travelling to the next county/state, or even across a border? A locally advertised car may not sound very interesting, but it can add to your knowledge for very little effort, so make a visit (it could even be in better condition than you expected).

Dealer or private sale?

Establish early-on if the car is being sold by its owner or by a trader. A private owner should have all the history, so don't be afraid to ask detailed questions. A dealer may have more limited knowledge of a car's history, but should have some documentation. A dealer may offer a warranty/guarantee (ask for a printed copy) and finance.

Cost of collection and delivery?

A dealer may be used to quoting for delivery by car transporter. A private owner may agree to meet you halfway, but only agree to this after you have seen the car at the seller's address to validate the documents. Conversely, you could meet halfway and agree the sale, but insist on meeting at the seller's address for the handover.

View – when and where?

It's always preferable to view at the seller's home or business premises. In the case of a private sale, the car's documentation should tally with the seller's name and address. Arrange to view only in daylight and avoid a wet day: most cars look better in poor light or when wet.

Reason for sale?

Make this one of the first questions. Why is the car being sold? How long has it been with the current owner? How many previous owners? Is it being sold because of a growing number of problems?

Left-hand drive to right-hand drive/specials

Only imported cars will be left-hand drive, and if a steering conversion has been carried out, it can only reduce the value – and other aspects of the car may still reflect the specification for a foreign market.

Condition (body/chassis/interior/mechanicals)?

Ask for an honest appraisal of the car's condition. Ask specifically about some of the check items described in chapter 7.

All original specification?

An original equipment car is invariably of higher value than a customised version. Well prepared 16-valve engines, turbo conversions, and factory recognised body conversions, however, can add a premium.

Matching data/legal ownership

Do VIN/chassis, engine numbers, and licence plate match the official registration document? Is the owner's name and address recorded in the official registration documents?

For those countries requiring an annual test of roadworthiness, does the car have a document showing it complies? (An MoT certificate in the UK, which can be verified on 0845 600 5977.) If a smog/emissions certificate is mandatory, does the car have one? If required, does the car carry a valid current road fund (tax in the UK) licence/licence plate tag? If so, when does it run out? Does the seller own the car outright? Money might be owed to a finance company or bank: the car could even be stolen. Several organisations will supply the data on ownership, based on the licence plate number, for a fee. Such companies can often also tell you whether the car has been 'written off' by an insurance company.

In the UK the following organisations can supply vehicle data:

HPI – 01722 422 422   DVLA – 0870 240 0010
AA – 0870 600 0836   RAC – 0870 533 3660
Other countries will have similar organisations.

Unleaded fuel

Cars fitted with a catalytic converter must run on unleaded fuel.

Insurance

Check with your existing insurer before setting out; your current policy might not cover you to drive the car if you do purchase it.

How you can pay

A cheque will take several days to clear, and the seller may prefer to sell to a cash buyer. However, a banker's draft (a cheque issued by a bank) is as good as cash, but safer, so contact your own bank and become familiar with the formalities that are necessary to obtain one.

Buying at auction?

If the intention is to buy at auction, see chapter 10 for further advice.

Professional vehicle check (mechanical examination)

There are often marque/model specialists who will undertake a professional examination of a vehicle on your behalf. Owners' clubs will be able to put you in touch with such specialists.

Other organisations that will carry out a general professional check in the UK are:
AA – 0800 085 3007 (motoring organisation with vehicle inspectors)
ABS – 0800 358 5855 (specialist vehicle inspection company)
RAC – 0870 533 3660 (motoring organisation with vehicle inspectors)
Other countries will have similar organisations.

6 Inspection equipment
– these items will really help

Before you rush out the door, gather together a few items that will help as you work your way around the car.

This book
This book is designed to be your guide at every step, so take it along and use the check boxes to help you assess each area of the car you're interested in. Don't be afraid to let the seller see you using it.

Reading glasses (if you need them for close work)
Take your reading glasses if you need them to read documents and make close-up inspections.

Magnet (not powerful, a fridge magnet is ideal)
A magnet will help you check if the car is full of filler, or has fibreglass panels. Use the magnet to sample bodywork areas all around the car, but be careful not to damage the paintwork. Expect a little filler here and there, but not whole panels. There's nothing wrong with fibreglass panels, but a purist might want the car to be as original as possible.

Torch
A torch with fresh batteries is useful for peering into the wheelarches and under the car.

Probe (a small screwdriver works very well)
A small screwdriver can be used – with care – as a probe, particularly in the wheelarches and on the underside, and any areas of severe corrosion – but be careful: if it's really bad the screwdriver might go right through the metal!

Overalls
Be prepared to get dirty. Take along a pair of overalls, if you have them.

Mirror on a stick
Fixing a mirror at an angle on the end of a stick may seem odd, but you'll probably need it to check the condition of the underside of the car. It will also help you to peer into some of the important crevices. You can also use it, together with the torch, along the underside of the sills and on the floor.

Digital camera
If you have the use of a digital camera, take it along so that later you can study some areas of the car more closely. Take a picture of any part of the car that causes you concern, and seek a friend's opinion.

A friend, preferably a knowledgeable enthusiast
Ideally, have a friend or knowledgeable enthusiast accompany you: a second opinion is always valuable.

7 Fifteen minute evaluation
– walk away or stay?

Having read chapter 5, you should now be prepared for the viewing. If the car fails this 15 minute evaluation, it's probably best to walk away, unless you want a project car. Buy the best you can afford, it works out cheaper in the long run.

Does the seller information match your expectations? Has the car been well looked after early in its life? My own car's service history covers 90,000 miles. Lots of receipts for parts and garage work are a good sign: look for cambelt changes, oil changes, and valve stem oil seal replacements. Most cars will have had many owners, with varying levels of care. Some will have had a hard life through over-enthusiastic driving, although, if regularly serviced, this is not normally a problem: avoid tired/thrashed cars.

If you know someone who owns a 205, ask them to go along with you. Owners' clubs can provide valuable information (chapter 16), especially if you're interested in a special edition or modified car. If you're competent, take a friend along to help: a second pair of eyes can be invaluable. Just make sure you're well informed and know what to expect.

This is what you want to see; lots of garage bills and receipts.

This guide will focus on the GTI, but makes special mention of the CTI where required.

Exterior bodywork
Due to the nature of these cars it's important to carefully check the panel and paint work for accident damage or repair. The body shape means it's quite easy to check panel alignment, and identify any damage/repairs. First, look along the bodywork for variations in colour, uneven paint (indicating filler), and distorted panels. Look for overspray on fittings (sunroof glide rails, door and window seals, trim, suspension, and engine components) indicating a budget job. If you find signs of repair, check it's been done professionally. Many insurance companies wouldn't pay for genuine panels, so check panel fit and shut lines carefully. Check that the bonnet, doors, and tailgate close easily and are a good fit all round (the fit will never rival a Mercedes, but should be reasonably good). Examine the wheelarches, and check the inner wings for signs of accident damage.

Next, open the bonnet and, again, examine the inner wings for distortion. Check that the bolts holding the tops of the wings are the same colour as the rest of the paint. Each bolt head should be stamped with an identical mark and show no signs of having been removed. The original slam panel (above the grille) should be black on phase 1 and late phase 2 cars, and beige/grey on the rest.

Cracks and rust can result from accident damage, very stiff suspension, or age.

The towing eye can be lost during a front-end repair, so check it's present. The lower part of the front wing, and the leading edge of the lower part of the door, should have anti-chip paint.

Look for structural repairs to the front chassis/under body. Chassis straightening equipment can leave imprints on the jacking points on the underside of the sills. Open a door, pull back some of the rubber seal, and lift the carpets, checking that the panels join correctly and there's no rust or welding repairs. Welds running across the floor from sill-to-sill indicate a 'cut and shut,' made from two write-offs – unfortunately all too popular in the '80s. If you're still unsure, look through the history, and contact previous owners to ask if there was any accident damage.

A single key should work all the locks (doors, rear hatch, petrol cap, and the ignition); if it doesn't, ask why. It may have been stolen/recovered, and the locks replaced, or it may have worn, or been damaged by thieves (being easy to break into, GTIs in particular were, and are, a prime target for thieves). Anti-scratch stickers can hide damage around the locks.

Rust

With a 6-year anti-corrosion guarantee from new, it's unusual to find any serious rot.

The chassis was galvanised in production, which is why so many survive, seeing-off their '80s rivals. Strangely, late cars are more rust-prone. However, even well looked after cars are now getting on, so check carefully.

If the front wings are rusty, they're probably not original. Check the front inner and outer wings and extremities for rust, and the panel supporting the headlamps. Although it's difficult to see behind the bumper, it's important to look behind the panel, and where it joins the inner wings.

Check the sill tops (especially between the sill and rear wing), and the bases of the B-posts, for signs of corrosion. The rear quarter panel and rear arches are also prone. The tailgate base, and around the rear screen, can rust if a replacement screen has been poorly fitted. The fuel tank sits across the car, creating a mud trap between it and the sills, so look there, too. Next, open the rear hatch, pull back some of the rubber seal, and lift the boot mat, checking there's no welding repairs or rust. Also check under the rear seats.

Check the inner wings from below and above. Note the beige/grey slam panel and body-coloured bolts on the wings.

Interior

Peugeots of this age are known for their flimsy interiors and switchgear, so don't expect German build quality! However, the interior generally survives well unless it's had a hard life, or is water damaged from leaky rear windows, sunroofs, and windscreens. Check for seat staining, and under the carpets for damp and rust. CTI carpets were bespoke, so aren't easily replaced – and being a soft top, it may have bleached considerably (although you could try carpet dye). Upholstery patterns varied throughout production, and all

Instrument panel torque screw should be present, especially in low mileage cars.

cloth-covered seats wore particularly badly, with replacements hard to find. Half-leather seats were more robust.

Unfortunately, GTIs were prone to having their odometers 'clocked,' so regard low mileage examples with suspicion: check it has a full service history to back up the mileage. Check for excessive interior wear: worn seats, driver's mat, and pedal rubbers – is the interior original? A shiny 'polished' steering wheel and gear knob could indicate a higher mileage.

Has the instrument panel been disassembled? Take hold of the instrument panel and check it doesn't move. Look for the torque screw, at the side of the panel (pictured): if it's missing, or has been replaced by another type, the instruments have been apart. Also look for fingermarks inside the instrument cluster.

CTI hood

Examine the condition of the hood and rear window for splits or damage, especially from thieves. Costs for replacement hood parts can seriously mount up, making it cheaper to buy parts secondhand, or even another car for spares! A new hood can cost over ●x400 (plus labour) to replace, and is difficult and time-consuming to fit yourself, especially if you discover the frame is damaged, so check carefully.

Check the operation of the hood mechanism. Power hoods should take around 15 seconds to complete their operation, and will only operate with the engine off. It will also fail to work if the oil warning light doesn't come on with the ignition (probably due to a faulty oil pressure sensor). Check also the condition of the window, door, and hood seals, and for signs of leaks (wet carpets and stained seats).

Electrics

Insurers require an immobiliser to be fitted to GTIs, so check it's present or pay a premium. An alarm is a good idea, too. Most were spliced into the existing loom, so check it's a professional installation by looking in the fuse box (located in the glove box), and behind the steering column under the dash. Check all the electrics work: some Peugeot electronic components can be very expensive (chapter 2).

Unfortunately, not all aftermarket immobilisers were installed neatly – more importantly, check it works.

Suspension

Peugeot's clever compact rear suspension beam design is also its Achilles heel; the bearings are prone to seizing, and are expensive to repair. Look at the rear of the car: it should sit level, with a small amount of positive camber of the rear wheels. Excessive camber (/ \), or one side sitting low, is a sign of trouble. Sit on the inside edge of the boot and bounce the car up and down: any creaking indicates a problem. If possible, jack up the car to see if the trailing arm is seized or has excessive play (both MoT failures). Being difficult to rectify, a reconditioned or good

Tired and worn rear suspension is difficult and expensive to replace; ensure you check it. (Courtesy Rob King)

secondhand unit might be a viable option. If the alignment of a single wheel is out, it may have been heavily curbed, and will need a new stub axle or trailing arm.

Next, check the front suspension using the 'bounce test,' by pressing down on each front corner: the suspension should be stiff with no creaking noises, and the shock absorbers should control rebound to a single, smooth movement.

Mechanicals
What condition is the engine bay in?

The overall condition is a good indicator of how the car has been cared for. Check the level and condition of oil on the dipstick: dirty oil or a low level indicates a lack of care.

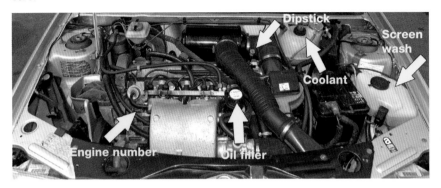

An engine bay this clean is a good sign.

Peugeot's XU engines have a proven reputation for reliability and long life (well over 100,000 miles) – provided oil and filter changes are carried out every 6000 miles. Engines can get a bit smoky with age, and the cylinder head and sump are prone to leaking oil, which slowly builds up and looks a mess.

Ask the seller about cambelt changes: it needs changing every 48,000 miles, the parts are cheap, but access is limited. If bought, invest in a set of ratchet spanners before tackling this job, and replace the water pump and tensioner at the same time.

The oil breather system is prone to condensation, causing a build up of 'mayonnaise' (emulsified oil) in the oil filler, especially on vehicles that do short journeys in the winter. However, don't rule out head gasket failure, which is more common on 1.9s: check for oil in the coolant and on the cap – but ensure the engine is cold first. Is the coolant the correct colour and level? A 50:50 mix is essential for protection from freezing and corrosion.

If you're buying a 1.9 GTi, check the engine number (located on the driver's side of the cylinder head), starts with XU9 (XU5 denotes a 1.6). If it's missing, look for an aluminium stiffening plate between the sump and block.

'Mayo' in the oil filler cap could be caused by condensation from short journeys – or suggest head gasket failure.

1.9 stiffening plate.

Later engine's numbers are stamped on a machined surface on the front of the block, at the flywheel end. Fuel injectors are another indicator: yellow on a 1.9 and black on a 1.6. If you're looking at a 16-valve or turbo installation, make sure you do your research and know what your looking at, or take someone along who does.

If it's an early non-cat 1.9 GTI, ask what fuel is currently being used. These cars require Super Unleaded (98 RON): poor fuel economy will result if Standard (95 RON) is used, unless the distributor is suitably retarded (although this inevitably reduces performance). I get an extra 50 miles from a tank using Super, so it's worth the extra expense.

Initial start-up

Always see the engine started from cold – be cautious if the engine is warm when you arrive. Ask the seller to start the engine. Some smoke on start-up is normal (and GTIs are known to have a rough idle), but it should only be 'tappety' for the first few minutes – have the valve clearances been neglected? If so, this can be a bargaining point, as it requires the camshaft to be removed to change the bucket shims.

Let the engine warm-up, listen for noisy ancillaries, and look for fluid leaks. Once warm, excessive smoke indicates a problem – a more detailed start-up procedure is in chapter 9.

Now's the time to decide whether to stay for a closer inspection, or walk away.

Don't let your heart rule you head

Don't let the seller influence or pressurise you into making a decision (take a friend and discuss); and, don't buy the first car you see – unless it's mint and the right price.

A good 205 GTI is one of the best handling classic cars you can buy, but check carefully before you do. (Courtesy Michael Cockbain)

8 Key points
– where to look for problems

Buying an excellent example like this one will save a lot of money in the long run.

Rust prone areas:
1. Check the panel supporting the headlamps and the extremities of the wings.
2. Check the sill tops, especially between the sill and rear wing.
3 Blocked drain holes in the door can encourage the bottom of the doors to rot.
4. Base of the B-pillars.
5. The rear quarter panel and rear arches.
6. The mud trap between the fuel tank and the sills.
7. A poorly fitted/leaking rear screen can cause rust at base of the tailgate and around the rear screen.
8. Cracked filler or rust above the rear quarter window.

Check under the rear seats: there is a water trap under the floor where three seams meet the rear crossmember. (Courtesy Mark Dixon)

Check carefully for frontal damage, poor quality repairs, and tell-tale corrosion.

Regard low mileage examples with suspicion: 'clocking' was common on GTIs, so check the paperwork, and the interior for wear.

Is it the right engine for the model? Beware of very smoky, tired engines.

Check the rear suspension is level, with no excessive wheel camber or seized trailing arms.

CTI hoods and seals are expensive to replace and can leak, so check carefully.

Damp interiors are common on GTIs – check for leaks from the sunroof, windscreen, and rear quarter windows.

9 Serious evaluation
– 60 minutes for years of enjoyment

Your potential purchase has made it this far – 60 minutes more is a small price to pay for future peace of mind. Even a really clean looking car can hide rust and other problems which may not have shown up on the initial 15-minute inspection, so it's definitely worth a more detailed examination.

Score each section using the boxes as follows:
4 = excellent; 3 = good; 2 = average; 1 = poor. The totting up procedure is detailed at the end of the chapter. Be realistic in your marking!

Red paint can fade particularly badly, and cannot be T-cut as it's lacquered. Note the difference between these two cars.

Distorted or misaligned panels could indicate the car has had accident damage/ repairs.

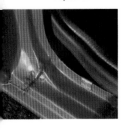

The bottom of the B-post is prone to corrosion ...

Exterior
Paintwork   ☐4 ☐3 ☐2 ☐1

Using a good light source, take a closer look at the quality of the paint and bodywork: has it been badly sprayed/repaired? If you spotted overspray in your initial inspection, now's the time for further investigation. A specialist can remove minor scuffs and dents, but patchy paint or poor quality repairs can be costly to correct. Paintwork is usually good, although lacquer can peel on the wings, roof, and bonnet. Red paint fades particularly badly. For more information on common paint problems refer to chapter 14.

Shut lines and panel fit   ☐4 ☐3 ☐2 ☐1

Having confirmed the car hasn't been in a serious accident, a more detailed inspection should now be undertaken. Peugeot's light, thin bodywork may improve handling and performance, but it's prone to dents. Check the panel fit/gaps, which may indicate accident damage or poor panel fitment. Identifying non-genuine front wings is fairly easy, as the panel fit varies enormously.

Doors, sills, and rear wings   ☐4 ☐3 ☐2 ☐1

Did the doors open and close easily during your earlier inspection? If not, they may be incorrectly adjusted or have been removed, perhaps because of a sill repair or an accident. Worn door-pins can cause the door to creak or drop, requiring greasing or replacement. Unless the drain holes are blocked, doors should be rust free. With the doors open, look for rust in the bottom corners of the door frames – a common problem area. Originally, there would be spot welds between the rear wings and

... as is the lower rear quarter panel and sill. (Courtesy Ross Obey)

the sill. Sitting in the driver's seat, look below the door mountings, and check the overlap of the front wing and sill; there should be no welding seams. If you're unsure, compare with the other side; if it's a different shape, it's not a genuine wing.

Genuine wings should have folded edges where they join the bodywork. (Courtesy Ross Obey)

Check the seam between the lower rear quarter panel and sill – it can be a serious rust spot. Peugeot used a large dose of seam sealer, but if it's cracked or the paint has bubbled, it can rot through from inside. Blocked sill drain holes cause similar problems.

Inner wing rot in the engine bay ...

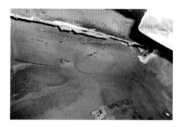

... and from underneath.

Also check below the headlamps.

Wings and bonnet

Look for rust and corrosion in the engine bay. Investigate both from above and below, to see if the inner wing is badly rusted. This could be difficult to spot during initial viewing, so remove the jack. Peugeot used a large dose of seam sealer here, too, between the inner and outer wings: essential to prevent the ingress of dirt and water.

Filler and cracks

Take the time to tap all the panels with your knuckles (or use a magnet), and see if you can find any filler you may have missed earlier. Check around the sills, wings, and doors, remembering a lot of filler was used in the panel seams during manufacture.

Bumpers and trim can fade, although can be revived with some work.

Exterior trim

Black or grey plastic bumpers and body mouldings are prone to fading with age and neglect, but can be restored with products such as Plasticare, a hot-air paint stripping gun (although only on some plastics), or a respray. Check the red pinstripe is present, as well as all badges: these are often stolen or missing, and the cost of replacement can rapidly mount up.

Wipers

Check operation. Worn wiper spindles cause a sluggish

action, and rear wash wipers are notorious for not working, usually due to bad connections.

CTI soft top and tonneau

Is the hood original or a replacement? Is it vinyl or the more expensive mohair? Check for rips, tears, fading, and shrinking. Windows can be replaced at a cost, but are prone to

scratches and cracks, and become opaque. The hood should have a separate rear window; if you need to change this, be aware that the zips can vary between hoods.

Check that the hood can be firmly secured by the catch on the top corners of the windscreen post. Does it seal properly on the top of the windscreen, and the tops and fronts of the doors? Old seals can increase wind noise at speed. Hoods tend to wear first at the hinge at the back, creating a leak, with water collecting under the seats. Drainage holes should also be checked to ensure

Check the drainage pipes on both sides which enter the rear inner wings ... (Courtesy Stuart Farrimond)

... and exit behind the rear valance. If they're blocked or cracked corrosion will quickly set in. (Courtesy Stuart Farrimond)

that they're clear. Check that the hood folds back behind the rear seats, and inspect the condition of the tonneau cover, if present.

Unfortunately, replacing a manual hood with a power hood requires a lot of work, as many parts aren't interchangeable.

Glass

Check for chips, cracks or scratches, and that the correct GTI bronze-tinted windscreen is fitted. Check for leaks and staining at the top corners of the windscreen, behind the sunvisors. Leaks can be temporarily fixed with a bead of windscreen or silicon sealant, but will require the removal, cleaning or replacement of the windscreen rubber. The window seal on the rear three-quarter window is prone to shrinkage, allowing water into the rear footwells: it will need stretching in a bucket of hot water or replacing. On GTIs, check the rear demister works.

Lights

If originality is important to you, check the correct indicators and rear lights are fitted. Cars from 1990 onwards had clear indicators and smoked rear lenses, which can be retro-fitted using a modified rear loom. Driving lights on the front spoiler

Late clear front indicators. See how vulnerable the front driving lights are to damage and corrosion. Notice the headlight protector.

Early orange front indicators.

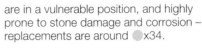

are in a vulnerable position, and highly prone to stone damage and corrosion – replacements are around ⬤x34.

Early rear lights.

Wheels and tyres
Wheel condition ☐4 ☐3 ☐2 ☐1
Curbed alloys can be expensive to replace, so are a bargaining point. Most owners have upgraded to the preferred 1.9 alloys, as it not only look better, but also gives greater tyre choice.

Late smoked rear lenses. Note the separate reversing lamp in the rear valance.

Tyre condition/rating ☐4 ☐3 ☐2 ☐1
Are the tyre/wheel sizes correct? (Check chapter 17.) Are all the tyres of the same specification and brand? Ideally, all four should be identical – or at least two on the same axle. The 205 GTI is a performance car, so tyres such as Toyo Proxes or Eagle F1s are a sign of a conscientious owner. Look at the tread depth and coverage, and check for cracks and bulges. Worn, mismatched or cheap tyres seriously compromise handling and safety. If the tyres are unevenly worn, suspect incorrect tracking or wheel alignment – or possibly worn suspension or steering parts.

1.9 alloy. Early 'phone dial' alloys were Speedline; later ones look very similar but were (allegedly slightly heavier) SMR.

The original 1.6 GTI pepper pot alloy. Some tyre centres may find it difficult to balance, as it has no centre cap.

Hub bearings and steering joints ☐4 ☐3 ☐2 ☐1
Jack up the front of the car, and put it on axle stands. Check all the suspension components are tight, and the trackrod ends, anti-roll bar, and drop links etc aren't worn. Grip the front wheel at 12 and 6 o'clock positions, and check for play in the bottom ball joint and wishbone bushes (you may need to use a pry bar). Have an assistant sit in the car and hold the steering wheel, whilst you grip the front wheel at 3 and 9 o'clock positions, and check for play in the trackrod end and/or steering rack. You may also feel play in the wheel bearing during these checks. Repeat for both front wheels. Spin the wheels, listening for rumbling noises indicating worn wheel bearings. Repeat for the rear wheels, which should spin freely, unless the brakes are binding.

The driver's seat bolster tends to wear badly – a good indicator of the mileage of the car.

Interior
The interior should be in reasonable condition, and late model 1.9 GTI interiors are sought-after.

Seats ☐4 ☐3 ☐2 ☐1
Cloth seats were particularly prone to wear. Leather seats

are preferable, but were prone to splitting at the seams, and the leather could crack if left untreated. The outer driver seat bolsters tend to wear and collapse – if you're good at upholstery, replacement bolsters can be sourced from a good condition base model passenger seat. The padding on the outer wing of the driver's seat can slip, too.

The seat lifting mechanism (allowing access to the rear) wears, causing the seats to become 'rocking chairs'. This is solved by tightening any loose fixings, and using wire as washers to remove excess play.

Leaking interiors quickly cause a soggy mess. Sourcing and fixing the leak can be time-consuming.

Carpets

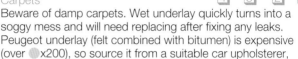

Beware of damp carpets. Wet underlay quickly turns into a soggy mess and will need replacing after fixing any leaks. Peugeot underlay (felt combined with bitumen) is expensive (over ●x200), so source it from a suitable car upholsterer, along with some sound-proofing material to stick to the floor (made a huge difference in my car). Red carpet shows the dirt, and replacements are expensive (●x150), although, being synthetic, it's easily cleaned, and GTI logo over-mats are still available.

Headlining

Headlining at the rear of GTIs can drop down, causing an annoying vibration at some speeds: gluing will be required. Also, check around the sunroof, and the top of the windscreen, to see if it's stained or damp, indicating a leak.

Sunroof (if fitted)

Full-length sliding glass sunroofs were common on GTIs (tilt sunroofs were after-market). The handle mechanism used the engine to create a vacuum for a watertight seal. To check it works, release the handle to de-pressurise the glass, listen for a hiss of air, and slide the sunroof back. Has the rubber seal failed? Pull the seal away, and look for rust and dirt trails indicative of a leak. Look for watermarks on the seats, footwell carpets, and around the handbrake. Blocked drain holes on the corners of the sunroof can be cleaned out using a long length of wire (the rubber drain pipes may also have perished). The handle can also leak, as the fibrous washers perish (these can be replaced with rubber ones). Finally, check that the sunroof closes easily, and – when the engine is running – raising the handle reseals sunroof.

Sunroofs are good in the summer, but are prone to leaking. Note the wind deflector.

Door cards

Special edition and CTI door cards are rare and expensive to replace, so check they're undamaged. CTI door cards in particular are unique, as they don't reach all the way to the windowsill.

CTI (and special edition) door cards are expensive to replace.

Door locks and handles
Having checked the condition of the door locks in chapter 7, now check the central locking works, if fitted. Early models operated from the key being used in the driver's door; later models used a notoriously unreliable remote fob.

Electric windows and manual winders
Check their operation. Sagging windows may indicate a damaged winder mechanism, which can rust, necessitating a replacement. Electric windows, where fitted, can become sticky, but silicon spray can free them up. Replacement electric motors are expensive.

Steering wheel
Black or grey leather steering wheels were standard fitment, and can become worn in high mileage cars.

Instrument panel
The '80s interiors tend to squeak and rattle with age, and the dashboard uses fairly cheap plastic that's prone to damage. Check for cracks and scratches, including around the stereo, which could indicate a break-in. Heaters are prone to faults, either running slowly or not at all. It's usually a fault with the control panel on the dash, or the resistor (or rheostat – located to the right of the blower under the passenger side dash), rather than the blower itself. Blowers can be become noisy, but this is easily fixed by lubricating the bearings with some 3-in-1 oil. Instrument function should be checked on the test drive.

Handbrake
The handbrake should operate with a maximum of 7-9 clicks: if it comes up too far the cable is stretched or needs adjusting. The 1.9 GTI's handbrake operates on the rear discs, and the mechanism is prone to seizing.

Boot interior
Check under the boot mat, and look for damp (there may be

Check that the jack and wheel brace are present – you may need them! Note the heavy duty jack fitted to all CTIs.

underlay sound proofing – a good idea). Leaks can come from the spoiler, window seals, rear wiper motor, and even the rear lights. The inadequate factory rear side panel speakers are often upgraded, fitting larger speakers in the rear parcel shelf. This can cause the shelf to become noisy, bouncing over bumps, and the hatch may be slower to open due to the extra weight, so check the condition of the gas struts.

The spare wheel is vulnerable to thieves: a cradle lock is a sensible investment.

Spare wheel and tool kit
Check the spare wheel underneath the boot floor is still

there. It's vulnerable to thieves, so it might be worth fitting a lock. The jack and wheel-brace are located under the bonnet, above the driver's-side wing – dealer fitted alarms moved the jack to the boot.

Under the bonnet (hood)

General impression ④ ③ ② ①
What was your earlier impression of the the engine bay? Were all the oil and fluids at the correct level? Leaks may indicate neglect or a tired car. Has the engine been rebuilt or steam-cleaned to hide leaks? Any doubts you had earlier should now be checked in greater detail.

Engine and chassis numbers ④ ③ ② ①
You checked the engine number in chapter 7, and if the engine is not original, proving the mileage of the replacement engine is very difficult, although condition, receipts, and a road test should help. A full list of engine numbers is given in chapter 17.

With the bonnet open, the chassis number can be seen beneath the windscreen on the driver's side, and the VIN number is on metal plate below; check it matches the paperwork.

Wiring ④ ③ ② ①
Peugeot electrics were never the most reliable, but does the wiring look like its been replaced? If so, it could indicate an engine swap, fire, or problems with the electrics.

Engine bay chassis number and VIN plate location.

Radiator and fans ④ ③ ② ①
Having earlier checked the coolant level, and for evidence of emulsified oil, now examine the condition of the radiator, and check for leaks. When you start the car, check the fans cut in and out when the engine is warm.

Hoses ④ ③ ② ①
Hoses could be over 20 years old: breather hoses can become blocked, split and crack, causing idling issues, and access is poor, making checks difficult. If you purchase the car, it's worth replacing them with higher quality silicone hoses (●x120). Check the cooling system pipes, including the heater pipes at the rear of the engine bay, and the matrix inside the car. Check adjacent areas for antifreeze or oil staining indicative of leaks or past problems.

Battery ④ ③ ② ①
Is it secured firmly and the right size? Is there a date mark? Are the terminals greased? It's common for the battery tray to corrode due to a leaking battery, but, bolting to the inner wing and gearbox mount, it's easily replaced.

Brake servo, master cylinder, and clutch ④ ③ ② ①
Check for corroded pipes, and leaks, especially the seal below the reservoir (some leakage is common). Low or dirty fluid is sign of neglect. The mechanical clutch's operation will be checked during the test drive.

Washer system

☒④ ☒③ ☒② ☒①

Early 205s have a single large washer bottle; in April 1986 it was moved behind the passenger headlight, and supplemented by a bottle in the driver's side of the boot. Look for leaks, and check the wiper/wash operation, including the GTI's rear wash/wipe.

Engine leaks

☒④ ☒③ ☒② ☒①

Investigate any oil leaks you found earlier, and assess their severity, and how much reparation is involved. Check under the car for drips and puddles of oil.

Engine mountings

☒④ ☒③ ☒② ☒①

Check for corroded and broken mounts, which may be more apparent on the test drive. There's one on the top of the gearbox, under the battery tray; one on the driver's side of the cylinder head, to the inner wing; and one under the back of the engine, mounting it to the subframe. The latter mount is prone to wear, and many owners have replaced it with an uprated item, although this increases engine vibration (a 306 TD mount is a good compromise).

Intake manifold and induction

☒④ ☒③ ☒② ☒①

Check the airbox is secure, as the mounts are prone to rust. Also, look for splits in the hoses which will affect running. If an aftermarket induction kit is fitted, check the filter is clean, and the cold air induction pipe is present.

Fuel-injection system

☒④ ☒③ ☒② ☒①

The Bosch injection management systems (LE2/LU2 Jetronic or Motronic 1.3) are relatively simply and reliable, but time-consuming to maintain. It's important to understand these systems to be able to identify any problems. Basically, the ECU controls a roller-type electric fuel pump in the fuel tank, providing fuel to the engine. Information is sent to the ECU via three main sensors, relaying engine temperature, throttle position, and the quantity of air entering the engine (AFM). The ECU then calculates injector periods using a predetermined fuel map.

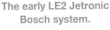

The early LE2 Jetronic Bosch system.

K&N kit has a 'claimed' power benefit, as well as an addictive induction roar, and removes much of the induction system, improving engine access.

LU2s were fairly basic, using the oxygen sensor in the exhaust system necessary for catalytic converters. Later cat-equipped Motronic cars were more advanced, with additional sensors to improve idling and emissions, including an oxygen sensor and a TDC (top dead centre) sensor for

You can spot a later, post-1990 engine from its coil, moved to the inlet manifold, and from its different thermostat block (hidden under the air flow meter) and expansion tank.

From 1992, when catalytic converters became mandatory, cars received the Bosch Motronic 1.3 system. Note the plastic inlet manifold. (Courtesy Stuart Farrimond)

The AFM with the case removed shows the spring and carbon track.

distributorless ignition – essential for more efficient fuelling.

From new, GTIs were known for a lumpy tickover when warm, due to its high-lift camshaft and light flywheel. However, idling and stalling shouldn't be a problem on a well set up and looked after car. If it is, it could be due to a poorly adjusted fuel-air mixture or idle speed. When warm, the idle should settle around 1000-1200rpm; any higher and suspect that the idle speed has been wound-up to mask problems. The idle mixture can be adjusted on the AFM using an allen key.

The AFM can cause lumpy idling, rectified by retracking the arm inside or finding suitable replacements – although new items are expensive (●x250). If you buy secondhand, check it hasn't been tampered with, as the coiled spring inside is calibrated during manufacture: unless you're a professional with a CO_2 meter, this shouldn't be altered. A faulty ECU temperature sensor (located under the distributor), or worn injectors, may cause over fuelling.

There may also be an air leak in the induction or oil breather system, causing lean running, blockage, or a build up of oil in the throttle body – a common problem. Poor electrical connections (ignition, earthing points, and the brown plug connector to the left of the battery tray) can be suspect, too.

If you buy the car, and experience very poor fuel economy even after you have checked everything, a tune-up on a rolling road is recommended. A faulty injection system will require a garage with diagnostic equipment.

Exhaust manifold and downpipes   ☒ ☒ ☒ ☒

Early exhaust manifolds are more prone to splits and cracks than the later ones with strengthening webs. Large cracks should be obvious, but can be difficult to see on the manifold underside. On start-up, listen for leaks or blowing, but be careful not to get burnt. If an expensive performance tubular 4-branch manifold is fitted, check it's not leaking at the prone flexible joint.

Steering rack   ☒ ☒ ☒ ☒

The steering racks are mostly manual and tend to have a hard life, due to enthusiastic driving, and wrestling with the heavy steering when parking. Check for play in the trackrod ends and the rack itself. A reconditioned exchange rack is ●x52 plus a refundable surcharge: a genuine rack (even a good secondhand one) is preferable, as it usually lasts longer. Power steering racks are a different design – check for fluid leaks from the ram and pipework.

Power steering pump/reservoir   ☒ ☒ ☒ ☒

Check the reservoir is full, and check for leaks around the pump (located by the alternator) and associated pipe work.

AC compressor ☐4 ☐3 ☐2 ☐1

Some models were fitted with air-conditioning, so check it still works. Check the reservoir is full, and for leaks around the pump and associated pipe work.

Turbocharged and 16-valve engines ☐4 ☐3 ☐2 ☐1

If you're determined to purchase one of these bespoke conversions, I recommend you enlist professional advice (or an expert from a club) for a closer look: some conversions are badly bodged (see chapter 12).

16-valve and turbo engines give a useful increase in power – just make sure you know what you're looking at, and that the running gear has been suitably upgraded. (Courtesy Mark Dixon)

Front suspension and brakes ☐4 ☐3 ☐2 ☐1

If you noted any noises during the initial bounce test in chapter 7, now's the time for further investigation. There should be no squeaks or knocking noises, usually caused by worn wishbone bushes, bottom ball joints, or faulty anti-roll bar drop links. If any suspension work has been carried out (especially lowering springs), get the tracking checked if you buy it. Also check there are no fluid leaks from the shock absorbers.

Brake discs can become rusty through lack of regular use. Scoring on the discs indicates worn pads, which can be investigated further on the ramp check.

Worn pads and scored discs may indicate neglect.

Rear suspension and brakes ☐4 ☐3 ☐2 ☐1

The rear suspension was checked in chapter 7, but will be investigated further in the on-ramp check (unless you want to use a jack/axle stands). Check the rear shocks for leaks; if it has rear discs, check as above. Rear drums are difficult to check without dismantling, but binding should be obvious.

Gearbox ☐4 ☐3 ☐2 ☐1

Access to the gearbox filler level bolt is difficult, so it will be checked later, on the ramp. Wear will be checked on the test drive, so, for now, just look for leaks.

Test drive (not less than 15 minutes)

The test drive is one of the most important tests, allowing you to assess the brakes, handling, and performance. Try also to listen for odd noises, and further assess any faults discovered earlier which you can use as bargaining points.

The test drive should use a variety of roads – twisty A or B roads are perfect for these cars, and will allow you to get a feel for the car and what it can do. Remember, like any performance car, drive it slowly at first, and get a feel for it before pushing on.

A test drive will not only give you a feel for the car, but will also show up suspension, brake, and engine problems. (Courtesy Dales Mills)

Cold start

The engine should start first time, and instantly – although it may require a little throttle from cold, and can be a little rough, initially.

The supplemental air device (SAD) can be troublesome. This allows extra air into the intake manifold, bypassing the throttle body. This extra airflow signals the ECU for additional fuel, causing the engine revs to rise, and prevents stalling when cold. As the engine warms, the SAD's bimetallic strip heats up, closing off additional airflow: if it's stuck or blocked with oil, it can also cause poor choke operation, leading to over or under revving.

Distributor wear is common, (particularly on the 1.9 GTI), and can also cause idle or stalling, and problems with cold starts. If the oil seal O-ring on the distributor has failed, it will leak oil into the cap, creating starting problems.

Was there any excessive smoke during the 15-minute evaluation, requiring further investigation? Ask a friend to rev the engine to 5000rpm – slowly at first, and then quickly – and watch the exhaust for smoke. Blue smoke can indicate a problem with the valve stem oil seals (which can be replaced without removing the head) or, more seriously, worn phosphor bronze valve guides (which is an expensive job). White smoke on start-up is normal, and is caused by condensation, especially in cold weather. Continued white smoke could indicate head gasket failure, evidenced by oil in the coolant, rapid coolant loss, and steam from the exhaust: check with a compression test. Black smoke is more serious, indicating worn bores and/or piston rings (although this will be more apparent when driving), so check the oil pressure, too.

Once warm (the fans have cut in and out twice), switch everything on, including headlights on main beam, heater blower, heated rear window etc: this is a good way to show up idle problems – especially when the cooling fan cuts in. If the fans don't cut in and out, suspect a faulty thermostat, or a corroded connection on the fan motor, which will lead to overheating problems in traffic.

On the test drive, check again for excessive exhaust smoke: ask a friend to watch as you drive away, or get them to follow you, as you may not be able to observe whilst driving. Look for dark smoke when coming on and off the throttle. Is the car sluggish at low revs, with white smoke (head gasket)?

Does the car stall when approaching junctions? This could be due to a low tickover, or injection system problems.

Handbrake (parking brake)

Check the operation of the handbrake, and that it holds on a slope.

Warning lights

With such a generous range of instruments, it's important to know what warning lights to look out for. When the heater hose burst in my own car the 'STOP' light came on (although the huge cloud of steam was also a clear indicator!).

Centre panel warning lights when lit indicate (top-to-bottom): Stop light: coolant temperature or oil pressure critical. Handbrake: handbrake applied/brake fluid level low (if it illuminates while driving). Battery: low charge. Coolant: level low. Sidelights: on. Main beam: on.

Please note that the following warning lights are not pictured:

Top right corner of the rev counter: catalytic converter overheating = exhaust, lit with a red light. Top left corner of the speedometer: front brake pad wear = yellow circle surrounded by dashed lines. Additional instrument information is covered later.

Clutch: operation and longevity

Is the clutch overly heavy? The cable can become stiff, and may snap. The point of take-up is a useful indicator; if it doesn't bite until the pedal is almost completely released, either the clutch is worn, or the cable needs adjusting.

Clutch slipping normally manifests itself in high gears, so when accelerating, check that the speed increases along with the revs. Try setting off from stationary in fourth gear; if the clutch isn't slipping, the engine should stall.

More seriously, does the clutch judder? If so, there's oil on the clutch from a failed oil seal – either from the engine, gearbox, or both. If the clutch release bearing is worn, it will make a whining noise when the clutch is released.

On early cars, the fuel-injection system can cause premature clutch wear (30,000 miles). Peugeot's attempt to improve economy (shutting off fuel when lifting off the accelerator, then switching it back on as the revs reach 1200rpm) causes shunting, requiring clever use of the clutch to avoid 'kangarooing'. The clutch on my early car has survived over 60,000 miles, but the problem is more pronounced in tired cars. A modified ECU can rectify the shunting, especially at part throttle, so it's worth checking if the car has one.

Manual gearbox operation (including reverse)

Generally, manual 5-speed gearboxes survive well, although gear changes are a little stiff when the engine is cold. This should become easier when warm, but still feel quite tight. If finding second gear is difficult, or crunches when warm, the synchromesh is wearing out – an expensive fix. Make sure that you can move up and down through the gears smoothly, and then shift down skipping a gear – from 5th to 3rd, for example.

The gear linkage is made of plastic cups and ball joints: it won't take much heavy use, and can wear (particularly the linkage next to the exhaust manifold). I recommend buying a rose-jointed set from an aftermarket supplier, although you'll need the car on a ramp or axle stands to change them. In the worse case scenario, the gear lever won't centralise, making selection difficult: the gear linkages can pop off too, which is a bit embarrassing in traffic!

Manual gearboxes with different ratios are interchangeable. The 1.6 gearbox gives better acceleration at the expense of top end performance. A 1.9 GTI gearbox = 60mph@3000rpm in top gear; if the engine revs more than this, it's a 1.6. Also, check the position of reverse to see if the correct BE-1 or -3 box is fitted (chapter 4).

Auto gearbox operation

Autos are generally reliable, but were mated to de-tuned engines, so don't expect GTI performance. Check the kickdown operation, that changes are smooth, and the gearbox isn't hunting for gears. Regular oil changes are essential for longevity, and low oil can cause problems with gear selection, as can poorly adjusted selector and kickdown cables.

Steering feel

The 205 GTI's suspension is straightforward, yet gives dynamic handling. On a straight road at a steady speed, check the car drives in a straight line: pulling to either side indicates a tracking problem. Suspension wear will be evident if the steering wheel wobbles whilst driving – possibly worn trackrod ends.

As with all test drives 'slow in, fast out' is a good rule when approaching a corner, particularly in a car that's not yours (yet), and that may have worn suspension. If you enter a corner too fast, and then lift off the accelerator completely, the back may step-out (oversteer) before you can catch it – you have been warned.

Steering should be sharp with no slackness, with small steering inputs resulting in a quick change of direction. Power steering, if fitted, should also give plenty of feedback, but, due to its design there's a tiny amount of initial play in the rack. It does, however, have an advantage when manoeuvring at parking speeds (particularly with 1.9 wheels), and catching oversteer, as it's a quicker rack. At slow speeds, manual steering will be stiff, so check for play in the rack. Incorrect tyre pressures can also significantly affect steering response (on turn-in, and especially when parking) or cause a harsh ride.

Brake operation

Servo-assisted braking should be very responsive. When braking from high speed, there should no pulling to one side, and it should be straight and progressive, with no wobble felt through the steering wheel. Problems here suggest a warped disc, seized calliper/wheel cylinder, or a seized brake compensator valve. The back end certainly shouldn't step out when braking. Unevenly worn or mismatched tyres can cause the car to slew under braking – so be careful.

Noises from steering/driveshafts

Find a car park or similar area, and put the steering on full lock. Drive slowly while listening for odd noises from the front suspension. A knocking noise indicates worn CV joints.

If the differential bearings are worn, you'll get wheel bearing noise when moving that doesn't change when turning the steering. These will need replacing, or risk collapsing and cracking the diff casing. The intermediate driveshaft bearing on the driver's side can sometimes be noisy, too.

If the diff itself is worn (possibly the diff pinion), you may hear a clunking noise when accelerating or decelerating in a straight line – don't confuse this with worn engine mounts. In addition, the car will probably pull strongly to one side when you accelerate, and to the other side when decelerating.

Noises from suspension and bearings

Creaking noises from the front (especially on bumpy roads) indicate worn wishbone bushes and/or ball joints. Bushes can be replaced (albeit a pig of a job), but the ball joints are integral, requiring a replacement wishbone. I recommend genuine Peugeot bushes (a kit is available): they last longer and aren't as harsh as aftermarket polyurethane bushes.

If the drop links fail, clicking or banging may be heard when driving over bumps. Anti-roll bar bushes are more robust (they're polyurethane as standard). Worn trackrod ends are common. Stiff or creaking steering is caused by seized strut top bearings: cheap, at ●x12 each, but time-consuming to replace, as you must dismantle the suspension strut to fit.

Creaking and cracking noises from the rear trailing arm bearings are expensive to fix (discussed in chapter 7). Knocking noises from the back? Suspect lose/worn rear beam mounts, lose anti-roll bar end plates, or worn shock mounts. Rumbling noises that increase with speed are due to worn wheel bearings.

Noises from engine, transmission, and interior

Listen for unusual noises from the engine: tapping (incorrect valve clearances due to wear), excessive rattling (from worn bearings), or banging. Minor noises should reduce once the engine is warm. Listen for transmission whine whilst driving, which could indicate worn bearings or gears. Worn engine mounts can be identified when accelerating or braking: you may be able feel engine movement – especially from the mounts on the driver's side.

Remember: it's easy to become paranoid about noises in an older car, especially with the (sometimes) noisy interiors.

Performance

Once the engine is warm, and you've checked the brakes are adequate, check the acceleration; it should be smooth and pull strongly to 6000rpm. Once it's up 'on the cam' – around 3500rpm+ – it should pull well, with no hesitation or misfires. Budget ignition parts can cause hesitation under load; branded parts are a good sign of care. Some throttle snatch and transmission shunt is normal.

Instruments

Check the instruments all function as detailed below:

Instrument cluster (89 GTI). Clockwise from bottom left: Fuel level; oil pressure; speedometer; centre panel (see warning lights); rev counter; oil temperature; and water temperature.

Oil pressure/temperature

Idling from cold, the oil pressure gauge (top left of dash) should increase to about three-quarters, and then slowly drop to half as the oil thins and the engine warms up. If not, suspect a faulty gauge, or a worn oil pump/relief valve spring – or simply the wrong viscosity oil. More seriously, it could be a worn engine: suspect bearings, bore wear, or even piston rings. The oil temperature gauge (top right) should also rise to about one-third when warm.

Water temperature

The water temp gauge (bottom right of dash) should rise to just under halfway. The cooling system rarely gives problems with overheating, as the system was designed to run in France's warmer climate. Check the two-speed thermostatic fan comes on when you stop. You may notice it stays on after the engine has been switched off; this is normal, but can be modified to prevent a flat battery. Cooling problems can be caused by corroded internals, a blocked radiator, a faulty thermostat, or incorrect anti-freeze mixture.

Switch operation

Check all the electrics work, and that the heater works efficiently (it's prone to poor

Behind the dashboard – what a mess! Corroded connections, faulty relays, and poor earths can be time-consuming to fix.

A session at the local garage may be invaluable at uncovering chassis and suspension problems. Few cars will be as clean as this! (Courtesy Michael Cockbain)

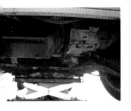

demisting). Early heaters/blowers were criticised because they could not be switched off. Also, check the front footwell and radio aperture, as the heater matrix can leak.

Electrical systems frequently give problems. Old wiring, damp and brittle connections, faulty relays – you may need to be handy with a multi-meter if you don't want to visit your local auto-electrician. A friend's 205 headlights used to flash intermittently when turning the steering wheel: a worn loom, earthing-out on the steering column, was the cause. Often, simply cleaning a poor earth connection helps, but a separate earth run may be required if the fault cannot be found (I have done this to cure sidelight problems). On the loom, the ends of the wires are numbered – useful if they're still visible (grease from your fingers does a good job of removing them). Cut back wires also lose their numbers, and are difficult to trace.

Ramp check

If you have access to a ramp or inspection pit, you'll benefit from a five-minute visual inspection of the underside. The best solution may be to take the car to an MoT vehicle testing centre (UK), and pay for an MoT (the examiner may allow you to join him, and may confirm your earlier findings). Please refer to the previous evaluation, and, in addition, check the following areas:

Chassis frame, floorpans
Take a look under the car to ensure there's plenty of underseal. Check the chassis for rust and damage, and check for dodgy welding repairs or the dreaded 'cut and shut.'

Engine and transmission
Check for oil and transmission fluid leaks. Check around the driveshafts for gearbox oil, indicating driveshaft oil seals need replacing, and look around the oil filter and oil cooler pipes (if fitted). Gearbox oil will tell you a lot about its condition. On a manual, you'll need to remove the filler level bolt to check the level – oil should run out if it's full. Automatics have a dipstick. A strong smell and dark colour indicates the oil hasn't been changed in a while.

Exhaust system
An early three- or later two-piece system ('89) will be fitted, depending on age. While the engine is running, check for signs of blowing, rust holes, and the condition of exhaust hangers. An emissions test will indicate the condition of the catalyst if fitted.

Oil leaks will be more apparent and easier to access on a ramp.

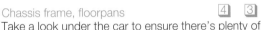

A repaired exhaust.

Brake lines

Check the brake lines are in good condition: the original steel brake lines are prone to rust, so copper replacements are a good sign. If possible, have an assistant apply the footbrake to put some pressure in the system, and check all wheels are held firmly by the brake. Look for bulges, and leaks from associated pipe work. Rear brake failure is often be due to corroded brake compensators or a sticking rear calliper. Replacing compensators is not a difficult job, but the steel pipes can rust and crack requiring large sections to be replaced. On the 1.9 GTI this may require removal of the fuel tank to gain access.

Rear brake compensator. There's one on each side on a 1.9 GTI. 1.6 GTIs have a different braking system, with the compensator located in the engine bay.

Fuel lines and fuel tank
Check that the fuel lines are in good condition, and aren't corroded or leaking. As discussed in chapter 7, check the mud and moisture trap behind the sill, by the petrol tank.

Cooling
Check the condition of the radiator and associated pipe work, looking for leaks. The steel water pipe, located behind the offside wheel, is prone to corrosion, especially if the plastic weather guard is missing (although it's cheap to replace, at ●x12). It's also worth checking the rear of the engine which can crack, leaking coolant.

Steering and suspension
In addition to your earlier inspection, check that the inner and outer rubber CV boots haven't split. This ultimately leads to CV failure (evident from knocking noises when going around corners), which you may have identified on the test drive. From below, check for leaks from the power steering and air-conditioning, if fitted.

If you suspect the rear beam is past its best, now's the time to check it. Jack the rear of the car on the ramp (most

Corrosion prone steel water pipe (this one is missing its weather guard).

ramps are now equipped for this), grip the rear tyre at 3 and 9 o'clock positions, and test for excessive play in the radius arm. Now jack up the radius arm, too, and check it's not seized (do this on both sides).

Check the inner and outer CV boots.   While on the ramp check the rear beam.

Summary
You should now have a really good idea of the condition, and (hopefully), the value of the car, and you know what needs to be done. If you don't buy the car, you can use the experience you've gained for the next vehicle.

I hope this information proves useful and that you're not put off: there are lots of good cars out there, but I have tried to identify the common pit falls and show the worse case scenarios. Good GTIs, in particular, are fantastic cars and offer a raw driving experience which, for the money, is hard to rival.

Evaluation procedure
Add up the total points.
Score: 268 = excellent; 201 = good; 134 = average; 67 = poor.
Cars scoring over 188 will be completely usable and will require only maintenance and care to preserve condition. Cars scoring between 67 and 137 will require some serious work (at much the same cost regardless of score). Cars scoring between 138 and 187 will require very careful assessment of the necessary repair/restoration costs in order to arrive at a realistic value.

10 Auctions
– sold! Another way to buy your dream

Auction pros & cons
Pros: Prices will usually be lower than a dealer's or private seller's, and you might grab a real bargain on the day. Auctioneers have usually established clear title with the seller. At the venue you can usually examine documentation relating to the vehicle.
Cons: You have to rely on a sketchy catalogue description of condition and history. The opportunity to inspect is limited and you cannot drive the car. Auction cars are often a little below par and may require some work. It's easy to overbid. There will usually be a buyer's premium to pay in addition to the auction hammer price.

Which auction?
Auctions by established auctioneers are advertised in car magazines and on the auction houses' websites. A catalogue, or a simple printed list of the lots for auction, might only be available a day or two ahead, though often lots are listed and pictured on auctioneers' websites much earlier. Contact the auction company to ask if previous auction selling prices are available as this is useful information (details of past sales are often available on websites).

Catalogue, entry fee and payment details
When you purchase the catalogue of vehicles in the auction, it often acts as a ticket allowing two people to attend the viewing days and the auction. Catalogue details tend to be comparatively brief, but will include information such as 'one owner from new, low mileage, full service history,' etc. It will also usually show a guide price giving you some idea of what to expect to pay, and will tell you what is charged as a 'Buyer's premium.' The catalogue will also contain details of acceptable forms of payment. At the fall of the hammer an immediate deposit is usually required, with the balance payable within 24 hours. If the plan is to pay cash, there may be a cash limit. Some auctions will accept payment by debit card. Sometimes credit or charge cards are acceptable, but will often incur an extra charge. A bank draft or bank transfer will have to be arranged in advance with your own bank, as well as with the auction house. No car will be released before all payments are cleared. If delays occur in payment transfers then storage costs can accrue.

Buyer's premium
A buyer's premium will be added to the hammer price: don't forget this in your calculations. It's not usual for there to be a further state tax or local tax on the purchase price and/or on the buyer's premium.

Viewing
In some instances it's possible to view on the day, or days before, as well as in the hours prior to the auction. There are auction officials available who are willing to help out by opening engine and luggage compartments and allowing you to inspect the interior. While the officials may start the engine for you, a test drive is out of the question. Crawling under and around the car as much as you want is permitted, but you can't suggest that the car you are interested in be jacked up, or attempt to do

the job yourself. Although you can open the bonnet and you can sit in the car. You can also ask to see any documentation available.

Bidding

Before you take part in the auction, decide your maximum bid – and stick to it!

It may take a while for the auctioneer to reach the lot you're interested in, so use that time to observe how other bidders behave. When it's the turn of your car, attract the auctioneer's attention and make an early bid. The auctioneer will then look to you for a reaction every time another bid is made, usually the bids will be in fixed increments until the bidding slows, when smaller increments will often be accepted before the hammer falls. If you want to withdraw from the bidding, make sure the auctioneer understands your intentions – a vigorous shake of the head when he or she looks to you for the next bid should do the trick!

Assuming that you're the successful bidder, the auctioneer will note your card or paddle number, and from that moment on you will be responsible for the vehicle.

If the car is unsold, either because it failed to reach the reserve or because there was little interest, it may be possible to negotiate with the owner, via the auctioneers, after the sale is over.

Successful bid

There are two more items to think about. How to get the car home, and insurance. If you can't drive the car, your own or a hired trailer is one way, another is to have the vehicle shipped using the facilities of a local company. The auction house will also have details of companies specialising in the transfer of cars.

Insurance for immediate cover can usually be purchased on site, but it may be more cost-effective to make arrangements with your own insurance company in advance, and then call to confirm the full details.

eBay & other online auctions

eBay and other online auctions could land you a car at a bargain price, though you'd be foolhardy to bid without examining the car first, something most sellers encourage. A useful feature of eBay is that the geographical location of the car is shown, so you can narrow your choices to those within a realistic radius of home. Be prepared to be outbid in the last few moments of the auction. Remember, your bid is binding and that it will be very, very difficult to get restitution in the case of a crooked seller fleecing you – caveat emptor!

Be aware that some cars offered for sale in online auctions are 'ghost' cars. Don't part with any cash without being sure that the vehicle actually exists and is as described (usually pre-bidding inspection is possible).

Auctioneers

Barrett-Jackson
www.barrett-jackson.com
Bonhams www.bonhams.com
British Car Auctions (BCA)
www.bca-europe.com or
www.british-car-auctions.co.uk
Cheffins www.cheffins.co.uk

Christies www.christies.com
Coys www.coys.co.uk
eBay www.ebay.com
H&H www.classic-auctions.co.uk
RM www.rmauctions.com
Shannons www.shannons.com.au
Silver www.silverauctions.com

11 Paperwork
– correct documentation is essential!

The paper trail
The best 205 GTIs and CTIs usually come with a large portfolio of paperwork, accumulated and passed on by a succession of proud owners. This documentation represents the real history of the car, and from it can be deduced the level of care the car has received, how much it's been used, which specialists have worked on it, and the dates of major repairs and restorations. All of this information will be priceless to you as the new owner, so be very wary of cars with little paperwork to support their claimed history.

Registration documents
All countries/states have some form of registration for private vehicles, whether it's the American 'pink slip' system or the British 'log book' system.

It's essential to check that the registration document is genuine, relates to the car in question, and records all details correctly, including chassis/VIN and engine numbers (if shown). If you're buying from the previous owner, their name and address will be recorded in the document: this will not be the case if you're buying from a dealer.

In the UK, the current (Euro-aligned) registration document is the 'V5C', and is printed in coloured sections of blue, green and pink. The blue section relates to the car specification, the green section has details of the new owner, and the pink section is sent to the DVLA in the UK when the car is sold. A small section in yellow deals with selling the car within the motor trade.

In the UK, the DVLA will provide details of earlier keepers of the vehicle upon payment of a small fee, and much can be learned in this way.

If the car has a foreign registration there may be expensive and time-consuming formalities to complete. Do you really want the hassle?

Roadworthiness certificate
Most country/state administrations require that vehicles are regularly tested to prove they're safe to use on the public highway, and don't produce excessive emissions. In the UK that test (the MoT) is carried out at approved testing stations for a fee. In the USA the requirement varies, but most states insist on an emissions test every two years as a minimum, while the police are charged with pulling over unsafe-looking vehicles.

In the UK the test is required annually once a vehicle becomes three years old. Of particular relevance for older cars, certificates include the mileage reading recorded at the test date and, therefore, are an independent record of that car's mileage history. Ask the seller if previous certificates are available. Without an MoT the vehicle should be trailered to its new home, unless you insist that a valid MoT is part of the deal. (Not such a bad idea, as at least you will know the car was roadworthy on the day it was tested and you don't need to wait for the old certificate to expire before having the test done.)

Road licence
The administration of every country/state charges some kind of tax for the use of

its road system, the actual form of the 'road licence' and how it's displayed varies enormously country to country and state to state.

Whatever the form of the 'road licence,' it must relate to the vehicle carrying it and must be present and valid if the car is to be legally driven on the public highway. The value of the licence will depend on the length of time for which it will continue to be valid.

In the UK, if a car is untaxed because it has not been used for a period of time, the owner has to inform the licensing authorities, otherwise the vehicle's date-related registration number will be lost, and there will be a painful amount of paperwork to get it re-registered.

Valuation certificate

For a restored or modified 205 in excellent condition, the seller may have a recent valuation certificate, or letter signed by a recognised expert, stating how much he, or she, believes the car to be worth (such documents, together with photos, are usually needed to get 'agreed value' insurance). Generally such documents should act only as confirmation of your own assessment of the car rather than a guarantee of value, as the expert has probably not seen the car in the flesh. The easiest way to find out how to obtain a formal valuation is to contact the Peugeot (205 GTI) owners' club (see chapter 16).

Service history

Most 205s will have been serviced at home by enthusiastic (and hopefully capable) owners. Nevertheless, try to obtain as much service history and other paperwork as you can. Naturally, dealer stamps or specialist garage receipts score highest points in the value stakes. However, anything helps in the authenticity game: ithe original bill of sale, handbook, parts invoices, and repair bills all add to the story and character of the car. Even a brochure correct to the year of the car's manufacture is a useful document, and something that you could well have to search hard to find in future years. If the seller claims that the car has been restored, then expect receipts and other evidence from a specialist restorer.

If the seller claims to have carried out regular servicing, ask what work was completed, when, and seek some evidence of it having been carried out. Your assessment of the car's overall condition should tell you whether the seller's claims are genuine.

Restoration photographs

If the seller tells you that the car has been restored, then expect to be shown a series of photographs taken while the restoration was under way. Pictures taken at various stages, and from various angles, should help you gauge the thoroughness of the work. If you buy the car, ask if you can have all the photographs as they form an important part of the vehicle's history. It's surprising how many sellers are happy to part with their car and accept your cash, but want to hang on to their photographs! In the latter event, you may be able to persuade the seller to get a set of copies made.

12 What's it worth?
– let your head rule your heart

Condition

If the 205 you've been looking at is in really bad condition, then you've probably not bothered to use the marking system in chapter 9. You may not have even got as far as chapter 9!

If you did use the marking system, you'll know whether the car is in excellent (maybe concours), good, average or poor condition, or perhaps somewhere in-between these categories.

Many classic/collector car magazines run a regular price guide. If you haven't bought the latest issues, do so now, and compare the suggested values for the model you're considering buying: look at the auction prices, too. Values have been fairly stable for some time, but some special edition models will always be more sought-after than others. Trends can change, too. Published values tend to vary from one magazine to another, as do their scales of condition, so read the guidance notes each provides carefully. Bear in mind that a car that's a recent show winner could be worth more than the highest scale published. Assuming that the car you have in mind isn't in show/concours condition, then relate the level of condition you judge the car to be in with the appropriate guide price. How does the figure compare with the asking price? Before you start haggling with the seller, consider what affect any variation from standard specification might have on the car's value.

If you're buying from a dealer, remember there will be a dealer's premium on the price.

Desirable options/extras

The top of the range 1.9 GTI is still the one the most desirable models, coming with many extras as standard (alloy wheels, electric windows, and leather seats). Factory-fitted options improved with later cars, and special editions, benefited from custom paint, interiors, power steering, and extra factory options, so they're worth looking out for – as is a power hood on a CTI. Further options such as metallic paint and factory-fitted bodykits allowed owners to individualise their car.

Modifications – the good, the bad, and the ugly ...

Without being exhaustive, here's what to look out for:

• A variety of suspension kits are available. Look for brands such as Bilstein, and Koni, although Peugeot still sell excellent shocks.

• A rebuilt rear beam is desirable as most are well past their best now, and uprated mounting bushes is a good handling mod, reducing lift-off oversteer. A similar effect can be achieved using a 309 GTI beam, which stiffens the rear suspension and widens track (the wheels are almost flush with the arches).

• 309 GTI front wishbones add negative camber, but its advisable to fit the 309's longer driveshafts, too, to avoid them popping out on full lock. A strut brace improves the rigidity of the front end.

• Swapping 14in rims to the better-looking 15in rims gives a better tyre choice, although it does affect the gearing.

• Power steering provides a quicker rack and is also ideal for track days – although some strong-armed drivers don't plumb-in the pump!

- A more robust aftermarket rose-jointed gear linkage and quickshift kit is also a good idea.
- Uprated brake pads such as Green Stuff, Mintex or Ferodo are adequate for most cars. Bigger and heavier callipers and discs from the other Peugeot models can also be fitted, although this is normally done in conjunction with serious engine tuning/conversion to maintain the balance of the car.
- Many cars are now getting on in years and have had a hard life. If the engine has had a partial or full rebuild, great, but check for receipts. Some cars have even been fitted with 16-valve or turbo engines.

Factory exhausts never looked sporty, so many owners have fitted aftermarket items – some more tasteful than others.

Undesirable features

Unless you plan on using your car for track days or competition, extreme tuning and handling modifications which improve horsepower and grip will often do little for driveability on the road.

Excessive lowered suspension creates a harsh ride, but 205 GTI road handling is better if slightly lowered by 40mm (although some ride comfort will be lost). Shorter suspension springs should, ideally, be matched with suitable shocks, and the rear beam lowered.

Large, loud exhausts can catch on speed bumps, and attract unwanted attention from the police.

Badly fitted bodykits can hide rust/problems.

Watch out for bodged engine swaps (including 1.9 in a 1.6 car, 16-valve, and turbo engines), paying special attention to wiring, engine mounts, pipework, and welding/bashing around the exhaust tunnel to make the manifold fit.

Striking a deal

Negotiate on the basis of your condition assessment, mileage, and fault rectification cost. Also, take into account the car's specification. Be realistic about the value, but don't be completely intractable: a small compromise on the part of the seller or buyer will often facilitate a deal at little real cost.

A 40mm suspension drop is plenty on a road car – Skip Brown or Eibach springs with suitable shocks work best.

13 Do you really want to restore?
– it'll take longer and cost more than you think

Fancy a project car? Consider the cost and the amount of work involved before deciding. Costs can mount and it's often cheaper to look for a more complete project, or even a restored car.

Perhaps you've seen a GTI that just needs a little work, or a CTI that requires a full restoration. The biggest cost in any professional restoration isn't the parts or materials involved, but the labour. Unless it's a rare special edition it may not be worth restoring, as there are so many good cars out there. Bodywork is considerably more expensive to restore than mechanicals so look for a good shell first and engine condition second. If you're determined to reshell a GTI, please be aware that non-GTI shells require extra work: smaller rear wheelarches require cutting; holes need to be made for trim clips; and engine mounting points may

need to be modified if it's not an XU-engined shell. Due to the cost and rarity of trim parts, I've known CTI owners buy two cabriolets just to make one good one!

Consider what the value of the car will be when restored, and what it will be worth to you.

Pattern panel fit varies enormously and can be troublesome and time-consuming to fix. (Courtesy Ross Obey)

DIY

Can you do-it-yourself? Do you have the facilities, time, and dedication? Restoring any car requires a wide range of skills – panel work, welding, prep-work, and painting. Even if you have the car professionally sprayed, you can still make a huge saving if you can do some of the work yourself: garage labour costs are high.

Can you rebuild an engine or gearbox? Research the cost: gasket sets, head bolts, service parts, and machining work soon add up.

Friends with the relevant skills/experience may help, but be realistic with time-scales: unless you're a professional, a body restoration can take you months instead of weeks.

Restoration projects

Before purchasing an unfinished restoration project, find out why the owner gave up. Did they lose interest, simply run out of money, or bitten off more than they could chew? What type of project car is it? If you think you can take it on, carefully

Rebuilt engines and restored engine bays add considerably to the overall condition of the car.

consider what you're getting into. Are all the parts there? Is any trim missing or damaged, and how easy or expensive is it to source? To what standard has the existing work been done?

A rolling restoration might be a more viable option, and a good bargaining point. Certainly, it will take longer and cost more in the long run, but at least you can enjoy your car, and work on it when time and funds allow.

Professional restoration

Professional restorations are expensive, so, before work begins, make it clear what you require – bare metal respray, new OE or pattern panels? Are they to remove the trim, interior etc, or will you do it?

Ensure you have detailed estimates, and are immediately informed if there's a dramatic change: you don't want a huge unexpected bill at the end. Visit them regularly to check progress, and take photos, which will be useful when you sell.

Does the company have a good reputation? Can you view previous jobs? Check they have worked on 205s before, and are, therefore, familiar with their construction and foibles.

Most good bodyshops have lengthy waiting lists: can you wait that long? You should expect some extra work and time, as the extent of the required restoration will not be obvious until the work begins.

Many owners have all the running gear refurbished, too, as it's a shame to fix rusty components to a refurbished shell. Professional engine and gearbox rebuilds will require a similar selection process, although it's often cheaper (albeit riskier) to buy a good secondhand unit.

Summary

Unless you truly wish to embark on a restoration, it's probably cheaper to look for a car that's already restored, or has been well looked after. Restoring a car can be harder than you think ...

A new soft top is often more cost-effective than repairing an old one.

14 Paint problems
– bad complexion, including dimples, pimples and bubbles

Paint faults generally occur due lack of protection/maintenance, or to poor preparation prior to a respray or touch-up. Some of the following conditions may be present in the car you're looking at:

Orange peel
This appears as an uneven paint surface, similar to the appearance of the skin of an orange. The fault is caused by the failure of atomized paint droplets to flow into each other when they hit a surface. It's sometimes possible to rub out the effect with proprietary paint cutting/rubbing compound or very fine grades of abrasive paper. A respray may be necessary in severe cases. Consult a bodywork repairer/paint shop for advice.

Cracking
Severe cases are likely to have been caused by too heavy an application of paint (or filler beneath the paint). Also, insufficient stirring of the paint before application can lead to the components being improperly mixed, and cracking can result. Incompatibility with the paint already on the panel can have a similar effect. To rectify it's necessary to rub down to a smooth, sound finish before respraying the problem area.

Sealant/filler can crack with age.

Crazing
Sometimes the paint takes on a crazed rather than a cracked appearance when the problems mentioned under 'Cracking' are present. This problem can also be caused by a reaction between the underlying surface and the paint. Paint removal and respraying the problem area is usually the only solution.

Blistering
Almost always caused by corrosion of the metal beneath the paint. Perforation will usually be found in the metal, and the damage will be worse than that suggested by the area of blistering. The metal will have to be repaired before repainting.

Micro blistering
Usually the result of an economy respray where inadequate heating has allowed moisture to settle on the car before spraying. Consult a paint specialist, but damaged paint will have to be removed before partial or full respraying. Can also be caused by car covers that don't 'breathe'.

Fading
Late phase 2 cars are more prone to fading due to Peugeot changing their paint. Red is especially prone to fading. In bad cases they can start to look pink or orange if

Red cars are particularly prone to paint fade and can go pink or orange.

subjected to strong sunlight for long periods without the benefit of polish protection. Sometimes proprietary paint restorers and/or paint cutting/rubbing compounds will retrieve the situation. Often a respray is the only real solution.

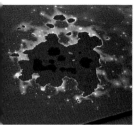 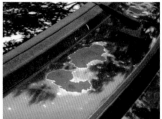 

Peugeot's lacquer can be prone to peeling, especially on the bonnet, roof, and wings.

Peeling
Often a problem with metallic paintwork starts when the sealing lacquer becomes damaged and begins to peel off. Poorly applied paint may also peel. The remedy is to strip and start again!

Dimples
Dimples in the paintwork are caused by polish residue (particularly silicone types) not being removed properly before respraying. Paint removal and repainting is the only solution.

Dents
205s, due their thin panels and lightweight construction, are prone to small dents. Fortunately, they can usually be easily cured by the 'Dentmaster,' or equivalent process, that sucks or pushes out the dent (as long as the paint surface is still intact). Companies offering dent removal services usually come to your home: consult your telephone directory.

Cars, like humans, are at their most efficient when regularly exercised. A run of at least ten miles, once a week, is recommended.

Seized components
Pistons in callipers, slave and master cylinders can seize. The clutch may seize if the plate becomes stuck to the flywheel through corrosion. Handbrakes (parking brakes) can seize if the cables and linkages rust. Drum and disc brakes may bind due to corrosion.

Engine bearings may be attacked by acid in old oil and, in severe cases, pistons can seize in the bores due to corrosion.

Rust can form on the brake discs causing them to seize solid. (Courtesy Trevor Fry)

Fluids
Old acidic oil can corrode bearings, but no oil means no protection, leading to rusted bores: check the oil colour and level on the dipstick.

Antifreeze is essential in these alloy engines; too little can cause cracks in the block or head, leading to head gasket failure and corroded waterways. Silt settling and solidifying in the cooling system, or a seized thermostat, can cause overheating.

Brake fluid absorbs water from the atmosphere, and should be renewed every two years. Old fluid with a high water content can cause corrosion and pistons/callipers to seize, and result in brake failure when hot braking components turn water to vapour.

Tyre problems
Tyres develop flat spots if left in the same position with the weight of the car on them for extended periods, resulting in (usually temporary) vibration. Tyres with walls that have developed cracks or blister-type bulges will need replacing.

Shock absorbers (dampers)
With lack of use, the shock absorbers lose their elasticity and can even seize. Seals can break down causing leaks, so it's worth checking each corner and doing the bounce test (as per chapter 9). Listen for creaking, groaning and stiff suspension – especially a seized rear beam. Some aftermarket suspension is adjustable, so it's worth checking the adjuster isn't seized.

In the interest of safety, old tyres should be replaced. (Courtesy Trevor Fry)

Rubber and plastic
Radiator hoses may have perished and split, possibly

Windscreen rubber can shrink due to heat and age; if it's not replaced it will eventually leak.

resulting in the loss of all coolant on your first test drive! Breather pipes are also prone to splitting, causing idling problems. Fuel pipes should also be checked. Fuel injectors can become blocked as petrol residue hardens over time, causing running problems. Window and door seals can harden, shrink, and leak – especially on CTI models and cars equipped with sunroofs – leading to wet carpets/seats and rotten underlay. Gaitors/boots can crack, which take time to replace. Suspension bushes can also harden and crack, as will wiper blades. Plastic bumpers, side and wheel arch trim can fade, although it can be rejuvenated.

Electrics
The battery will be of little use if it hasn't been charged. Electrical connectors commonly rust and corrode, causing earthing/grounding problems, and will need disconnecting and cleaning with emery paper or a file and contact cleaning fluid. Contacts should then be protected with electric contact spray (or Vaseline on battery terminals). Wiring insulation can also harden and fail, while sparkplug electrodes, dizzy cap, and rotor arm will often have corroded in an unused engine.

Rotting exhaust system
When a car isn't used, exhaust systems corrode very quickly from the inside (if you're lucky it might be stainless steel). The rubber exhaust hangers may also have failed.

Hoods/folding soft top
If the car has been left standing and gotten wet, the hood may have moss growth or rot.

Unwanted visitors
If the car has stood for a long period of time check for insects and rodents which can do untold damage. Also check for signs of a break in – is the stereo present? Are the door locks damaged?

Check if the car you're viewing has been in regular use. (Courtesy Dale Mills)

16 The Community

– key people, organisations and companies in the 205 world

Clubs/websites

205 GTI Drivers Forum
An invaluable free web resource and community focusing on maintenance and modification – everything you need to know!
http://forum.205gtidrivers.com/
www.205gtidrivers.com

205 GTI 1FM dedicated website
http://www.205gti1fm.co.uk/

205 GTI Peugeot part numbers online
www.stuartmcguire.co.uk/pug/

Club Peugeot UK
The oldest existing Peugeot club in the UK.
www.clubpeugeotuk.org

Mac's Peugeot Site
www.205GTI.com

Peugeot GTI Autosport Club
www.peugeot-GTI.net/

Peugeot Sport Club/ Peugeot Sport Official Owners' Club
PO Box 1410, Coventry, CV3 2WS
Tel: 0845 6443107 or 0845 1249560
www.peugeotsportclub.com
www.psooc.com

Specialists/motorsport
I am not endorsing or associated with any of the companies listed below, but I hope you find them useful.

Autofive – 205 GTI parts specialist
Harcourt St. Walkden, Manchester, England, M28 3GN
Tel: 01204 579599
www.autofive.co.uk

Baker Bushes & Mountings
Performance bushes, mountings, and silicone hoses
Tel. 07870 934034
www.bakerbm.com

BAS International
Cabriolet soft tops, car trimmings, and carpets
10-13, Llantarnam Park Ind Est Cwmbran, S Wales NP44 3AX
Tel: 01633 873664
www.car-hood.co.uk

Bypartsbuy (Autospares Sutton Ltd)
OE Arvin/Timax exhaust stockist
70-72 Acton Road, Long Eaton, Nottingham NG10 1FR
Tel: 0115 9835280
www.buypartsby.co.uk

Constella Tuning
Stockist of uprated gear linkage
24 Loughborough Rd, Shepshed, Leics LE12 9DN
Tel: 01509 507341
www.constella.co.uk

Dimma (Europe)
www.dimmadesign.com/en/
presentation.html

Ecosse Peugeot Specialists
Bo'mains Industrial Estate, Linlithgow Road, Bo'ness, EH51 0QG
Tel:01506 516106
www.ecosse-peugeot.co.uk

LAD Motorsport
Unit 1 Woodgate Park, White Lund Industrial Estate, Morecambe, Lancs. LA3 3PS
Tel: 01524 62748
www.ladmotorsport.co.uk

Neat Car Parts (Neat Autos Ltd)
OE Arvin/Timax exhaust stockist
Maksons House, 52 Station Road, West
Drayton, Middlesex UB7 7BT
TEL: 01895 90 70 50
www.parts4peugeot.com

Pugspares
www.pugspares.co.uk

Peugeot Sport Special Tuning
Performance and competition parts
PO Box 25, Humber Road, Coventry
CV3 1BD
Tel: 01203 884677
www.specialtuninguk.co.uk

Peugeot UK (parts desk)
Tel: 0845 200 1234 (to find your nearest
dealer)

Pug Performance
Hermitage Farm, Alton, Hampshire
GU34 3PU
Tel: 01420 587377

Pug Racing
Road, track, race, restoration services &
bodyshop
www.PugRacing.com
Tel: 01425 655109

Puma Racing
High performance engine building
www.pumaracing.co.uk

Shenpar Competitions
r/o 1 Potter Street, Melbourne,
Derbyshire. DE73 8DW
Tel: 01332 862901
www.shenpar.com

Skip Brown Cars
Peugeot Talbot performance specialists.
Ridley Green, Tarporley, Cheshire, CW6
9RY
Tel: 01829 720492
www.skipbrowncars.com

Taylor Engineering
Peugeot performance parts
http://www.taylor-eng.com/index.html

Turbo Technics
Turbocharger specialists
2 Sketty Close, Brackmills,
Northampton, NN4 7PL United Kingdom
Tel: 01604 705050
www.turbotechnics.com

Books
Improve and Modify Peugeot 205 by
Lindsay Porter, Dave Pollard
Haynes Publishing
ISBN: 978-0854298334

*Peugeot 106, 205, 206, 306 Workshop
Manual* (Lindsay Porter's Colour
Manuals)
by Ivor Carroll, Bob Cooke, Lindsay
Porter, Jim Tyler
Porter Publishing Ltd
ISBN: 978-1899238453

*Peugeot 205 GTI: The Enthusiast's
Companion* by Ray Hutton
Motor Racing Publications Ltd
ISBN: 978-0947981181

*Peugeot 205 Petrol (1983-1997) Service
and Repair Manual* (Haynes Service and
Repair Manuals) by AK Legg & John S
Mead
Haynes Publishing
ISBN: 978-1859607695

*Sporting Peugeot 205s: A Collectors
Guide* by Dave Thornton
Motor Racing Publications
ISBN: 978-1899870196

Peugeot 205 T16 (Rally Giants Series)
by Graham Robson
Veloce Publishing Ltd
ISBN: 9781845841294

17 Vital statistics
– essential data at your fingertips

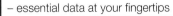

205 production figures

Year	GTI	CTI (cabriolets)	All models
1983	0	0	2883
1984	1874	0	19,670
1985	4971	0	30,842
1986	7378	427	39,188
1987	9477	582	49,127
1988	10,933	1020	54,147
1989	10,240	1070	52,740
1990	8324	1274	50,205
1991	5429	866	46,615
1992	2498	549	34,045
1993	521	434	23,065
1994	8	11	10,694
1995	0	0	9032
1996	0	0	3046
Total	61,653	6233	425,299

Source: www.205gtidrivers.com

205 GTIs sales peaked in 1988, accounting for a massive 20 per cent of total 205 UK sales.

205 GTI 1.6
Engine: Water-cooled four-cylinder, five-bearing aluminium alloy block (with wet liners). Aluminium alloy cylinder head, single overhead camshaft driven by toothed belt.

1984-1986 (XU5J-180A) Bosch Multipoint LE2 Jetronic fuel-injection system. 1580cc; bore 83mm; stroke 73mm; CR 10.2:1. Power: 105bhp at 6250rpm; 99lbf/ft at 4000rpm; max speed 118mph; 0-60mph 9.5 seconds; fuel economy (combined): 32mpg.

1986-1992 (XU5JA-B6D) Bosch Multipoint LE2 Jetronic fuel-injection system. 1580cc; bore 83mm; stroke 73mm; CR 9.8:1. Power: 115bhp at 6250rpm; 98lbf/ft at 4000rpm; max speed 121.7mph; 0-60mph 9.1 seconds; fuel economy (combined): 31mpg.

Drive/transmission: Front-wheel drive. Five-speed synchromesh transmission.
Gear ratios (mph per 1000rpm): 1st 3.31 (4.9); 2nd 1.88 (8.6); 3rd 1.36 (11.9); 4th 1.07 (15.2); 5th 0.87 (18.7). Final-drive: 4:06:1.
Clutch: Diaphragm spring, single dry plate, cable-operated clutch with 200mm diameter drive plate.
Suspension: Front: Independent with MacPherson struts, coil springs, proper

lower wishbones and anti-roll bar attached to strut via drop-link at each end. Rear: Independent trailing radius arms, transverse torsion bars, telescopic dampers and anti-roll bar.

Steering: Rack and pinion, 3.8 turns from lock to lock (power assisted 3.2).

Brakes: Front-rear dual circuit hydraulic with vacuum servo assistance. Inertia compensator valve fitted between front and rear brake lines. Cable-operated mechanical handbrake on rear wheels.

Front: 247mm (9.7in) diameter ventilated discs with Bendix or Girling single piston sliding caliper. Rear: 180mm (7.1in) self-adjusting drums with leading and trailing shoes.

Wheels: 5.5J-14in-diameter cast-alloys; 185/60HR-14 tyres, 29psi (2bar) front and rear.

Capacities: Fuel: 50lt (11 gallons); coolant: 6.5lt (11.5 pints); engine oil: 5lt (8.8 pints); manual transmission oil: 2lt (3.5 pints).

Dimensions: Length: 3706mm (145.9in); width: 1572mm (61.9in); height: 1354mm (53.3in); weight: 850kg (1874lb).

205 GTI 1.9 (as per 1.6 GTI with the following exceptions)

Engine: 1986-1992 (XU9JA - D6B) Bosch Multipoint LE2 injection system* 1905cc; bore 83mm; stroke 88mm; CR 9.6:1. Power: 130bhp at 6000rpm; 119lbf/ft at 4750rpm; 0-60 in 7.8 seconds; max speed 127mph (204km/h); fuel economy (combined): 30mpg.

1992-1994 (XU9JA/Z-DKZ) Bosch Multipoint Motronic M1.3 fuel-injection 1905cc; bore 83mm; stroke 88mm; CR 9.2:1. Power: 122bhp at 6000rpm; 101lbf/ft at 4000rpm; 0-60 in 8.5 seconds; max speed 125mph (201km/h); fuel economy (combined): 29mpg (CAT).

Gear ratios: (mph per 1000rpm): 1st 2.92 (6.2); 2nd 1.85 (9.8); 3rd 1.36 (13.3); 4th 1.07 (16.9); 5th 0.86 (20.9). Final-drive: 3:69:1.

Brakes: Larger front calliper, diagonal dual-circuit hydraulics and vacuum servo assistance with pressure compensator valves fitted between front and rear brake lines.

Front: 247mm (9.7in) diameter ventilated discs with Bendix or Girling single piston sliding caliper (larger than 1.6).

Rear: 247mm (9.7in) solid discs on 1.9 with Bendix single piston sliding caliper.

Wheels: 6.5J-15in-diameter cast-alloys; 185/55HR-15 tyres, 29psi (2bar) front and rear (195/50HR-15 are a common upgrade).

Dimensions: Length: 3706 mm (145.9in); width: 1572 mm (61.9in); height: 1354mm (53.3in); weight: 875kg (1929lb).

205 CTI (as per 1.6 GTI with the following exceptions)

Engine: 1984-1991 (XU5J B6D) Bosch Multipoint LE2 Jetronic fuel-injection system. 1580cc. 0-60 in 10.1 seconds, max speed 115mph (185km/h); fuel economy (combined): 30mpg.

1991-1994 (XU9JI/DFZ) Bosch Multipoint LU2 Jetronic fuel-injection 1905cc; bore 83mm; stroke 88mm; CR 8.4:1.
105bhp at 6000rpm; 103b/ft at 4000rpm. 0-60 in 10.6 seconds; top speed 115mph (185km/h); fuel economy (combined): 27mpg (CAT).

Suspension: Softer suspension than GTIs, similar setup to the XS model with the front anti-roll bar integral with the track control arms.

Dimensions: length: 3706mm (145.9in); width: 1590mm (62.6in); height: 1382mm (54.4in); weight 935kg (2062lb).

Special editions
Vital statics are as above unless otherwise stated. Further information is given in chapter 4.

Miami blue & Sorrento green Limited Edition – 600 Miami blue 'Limited Edition' (300 1.6 GTI; 300 1.9 GTI) and 600 Sorrento green 'Limited Edition' (300 1.6 GTI; 300 1.9 GTI) produced.
Griffe – 3000 produced for mainland Europe, with a small number imported to the UK.
Gentry – 300 models produced. Engine: XU9J1/Z (DFZ) LU2-Jetronic Multipoint Fuel-injection 1.9 105bhp engine, and automatic gearbox. CR 8.4:1. Fuel economy (combined): 27mpg (CAT).
25 'Radio 1FM' models – Only 25 made!
1.9 GTI Export Automatic – 150 produced. Engine: XU9J1/Z (DFZ) LU2-Jetronic Multipoint Fuel-injection 1.9 105bhp engine, and an automatic gearbox. CR 8.4:1. Fuel economy (combined): 27mpg (CAT).

After market conversions
Turbo Technics and Dimma conversions: estimate 100-200 models).

Codes & chassis numbers
VF3XXXXXX00000000 (XXXXXX is the manufacturer code)

Badge	Years	Capactiy	Max Power	Engine Type/No	Manufacturer code
205 GTI 1.6	84-86	1580cc	105bhp/75kW	XU5J	741C66
205 GTI 1.6	86-06/87	1580cc	115bhp/85kW	XU5JA	741C66
205 GTI 1.6	07/87-92	1580cc	115bhp/85kW	XU5JA	20CB62
205 GTI 1.9	02/86- 06/87	1905cc	130bhp/96kW	XU9JA/D6B	741C86
205 GTI 1.9	07/87-07/92	1905cc	130bhp/96kW	XU9JA/D6B	20CD62
205 GTI 1.9	07/92-96	1905cc CAT	122bhp/90kW	XU9JAZ/DKZ	20CDK2
205 GTI 1.9 Japanese export	Circa 92* (K plate)	1905cc CAT	105bhp/75kW	XU9J1/DFZ*	20CDF2
205 CTI	03/86 - 06/87	1580cc	115bhp/83kW	XU5JA	741B66
205 CTI	07/87-06/92	1580cc	115bhp/83kW	XU5JA	20DB62
205 CTI	07/92-96	1905cc CAT	105bhp/75kW	XU9J1/DFZ	20DDF2

Source: www.205gtidrivers.com   **amended by author*

The **Essential** Buyer's Guide™ series

More on the way!

£9.99*/$19.95*

*prices subject to change, p&p extra.
For more details visit www.veloce.co.uk or email info@veloce.co.uk

Call Us: 01895 907050

NEAT
www.neatcarparts.co.uk

Peugeot and Citroen car parts specialist

Star Item

PEUGEOT 407 307 2.0
HDI TURBO GARRETT
TURBO 037RK8 NEW

749.99
15days 3:41.09 left

Shop Search

Search

Shop Categories

Other
PEUGEOT 106
PEUGEOT 107
ABS SENSORS
ABS, SRS & SAFETY BELTS
ALTERNATOR & BATTERIES
BODY PANELS + BADGES
BRAKING + BRAKE HYDRAULICS
BUMPERS
CAR MATS
CLUTCH FORKS
CLUTCHES + FLYWHEEL KITS
COOLING &AIRCON
CRANKSHAFT PULLEYS
DOOR HANDLES
DOOR MIRRORS & GLASSES
DRIVE BELT TENSIONERS
ENGINE MOUNTINGS
ENGINE MOUNTS
ENGINE OIL CAPS
ENGINE OILS
ENGINE PARTS
EXHAUSTS
FAN-DRIVE, ALTERNATOR BELTS
FILTERS & SERVICE PARTS

Welcome to my eBay Shop. We are a French Car Parts specialists including Peugeot and Citroen Vehicles, we have a large range of parts and accessoires. We pride ourself on supplying the correct part the first. Please add me to your list of favourite sellers and come again. Thank you for your business

Search For Parts

-- Select ▼   -- Select ▼
-- Select Part --   ▼
GO

View as: Gallery   Sort by: Time: ending soonest

Postage to UK

Peugeot 205 305 306 309 405 406 Glow Plugs x4 BARGAIN
Buy It Now   £14.50
Postage: +£3.00
Time left: **4m**

WASHER PUMP TWIN OUTLET FOR CITROEN XANTIA 91 CHEAPEST
Buy It Now   £5.49
Postage: +£2.24
Time left: **4m**

WASHER PUMP TWIN OUTLET FOR PEUGEOT 806 93 643460
Buy It Now   £5.49
Postage: +£2.24
Time left: **4m**

INDICATOR LIGHT SWITCH FOR PEUGEOT 406 806 625354
Buy It Now   £45.00
Postage: +£4.99
Time left: **4m**

RENAULT MEGANE WASHER PUMP 91-98 TWIN OUTLET CHEAPEST
Buy It Now   £5.49
Postage: +£2.24
Time left: **4m**

PEUGEOT PARTNER SERVICE PARTS AIR+OIL+FUEL FILTERS +OIL
Buy It Now   £29.99
Postage: +£9.99
Time left: **4m**

Ending Soon

WASHER PUMP TWIN OUTLET FOR CITRION XANTIA 91 CHEAPEST
5.49
2m ins 44seconds left

WASHER PUMP TWIN OUTLET FOR PEUGEOT 806 93 643460
5.49
2m ins 50seconds left

INDICATOR LIGHT SWITCH FOR PEUGEOT 406 806 625354
45.00
2m ins 57seconds left

RENAULT MEGANE WASHER PUMP 91-98 TWIN OUTLET CHEAPEST
5.49
3m ins 01seconds left

PEUGEOT PARTNER SERVICE PARTS AIR+OIL+FUEL FILTERS
29.99
3m ins 04seconds left

NEAT car parts   (Neat Autos Ltd) Maksons House, 52 Station Road, West Drayton, Middlesex UB7 7BT 01895 90 70 50

Megan

Megan. Sales Clerk. Adrian Flux.

I'm as passionate about Peugeots as you are,
which is why I think you'll love our insurance deals.

Adrian Flux Insurance Services has been built around
the enthusiast markets and understands that people who are
passionate about their cars take good care of them. Because
we share your enthusiasm we offer fantastic, tailor-made
insurance deals based on your own personal driving history
and requirements. Call us today to obtain a no obligation
quote for your Peugeot 205 GTi.

FREEPHONE 0800 089 0035

Quoteline hours: Mon to Fri 9am-7pm | Sat 9am-4pm

adrianflux.co.uk

Authorised and regulated by the Financial Services Authority.

ADRIAN FLUX

Index